THE WAY WE GET BY

"It's sexy, it's starry . . . dangerously irres

"*The Way We Get By* has an unexpectec

"*The Way We Get By* feels like a refreshingly sunnier and more hopeful LaBute, with moments that feel suspiciously like giddy joy."
—**Sara Vilkomerson**, *Entertainment Weekly*

"Viscerally romantic, almost shockingly sensitive, even, dare we say it, sweet . . . LaBute . . . dares here to explore less obviously explosive territory. Yet, somehow, this daring feels deep." —**Linda Winer**, *Newsday*

THE MONEY SHOT

"A wickedly funny new comedy." —**Jennifer Farrar**, The Associated Press

"An acid-tongued showbiz satire." —**Scott Foundas**, *Variety*

"Fresh, joyously impolite . . . a good and mean little farce."
—**Linda Winer**, *Newsday*

"100 minutes of rapid-fire bursts of raucous laughter."
—**Michael Dale**, *BroadwayWorld*

"Packs a stunning amount of intelligence into 100 minutes of delectable idiocy."
—**Hayley Levitt**, *TheaterMania*

"Consistently entertaining . . . To his credit, LaBute does not aim for the obvious metaphor: in showbiz, everyone gets screwed. He is more concerned with amusing us." —**Brendan Lemon**, *Financial Times*

REASONS TO BE HAPPY

"Mr. LaBute is more relaxed as a playwright than he's ever been. He is clearly having a good time revisiting old friends . . . you're likely to feel the same way . . . the most winning romantic comedy of the summer, replete with love talk, LaBute-style, which isn't so far from hate talk . . ."
—**Ben Brantley**, *The New York Times*

"These working-class characters are in fine, foul-mouthed voice, thanks to the scribe's astonishing command of the sharp side of the mother tongue. But this time the women stand up for themselves and give as good as they get."
—**Marilyn Stasio**, *Variety*

"LaBute has a keen ear for conversational dialogue in all its profane, funny and inelegant glory." —**Joe Dziemianowicz**, *New York Daily News*

"LaBute . . . nails the bad faith, the grasping at straws, the defensive barbs that mark a tasty brawl." —**Elisabeth Vincentelli**, *New York Post*

"Intense, funny, and touching . . . In following up with the lives of his earlier characters, LaBute presents another compassionate examination of the ways people struggle to connect and try to find happiness."

—**Jennifer Farrar**, The Associated Press

"Terrifically entertaining."   —**Philip Boroff**, *Bloomberg*

"A triumph . . . always electric with life. LaBute has a terrific way of demonstrating that even in their direst spoken punches . . . fighting lovers are hilarious. . . . completely convincing."   —**David Finkle**, *Huffington Post*

REASONS TO BE PRETTY

"Mr. LaBute is writing some of the freshest and most illuminating American dialogue to be heard anywhere these days . . . *Reasons* flows with the compelling naturalness of overheard conversation. . . . It's never easy to say what you mean, or to know what you mean to begin with. With a delicacy that belies its crude vocabulary, *Reasons to be Pretty* celebrates the everyday heroism in the struggle to find out."   —**Ben Brantley**, *The New York Times*

"There is no doubt that LaBute knows how to hold an audience. . . . LaBute proves just as interesting writing about human decency as when he is writing about the darker urgings of the human heart."   —**Charles Spencer**, *Telegraph*

"Funny, daring, thought-provoking . . ."   —**Sarah Hemming**, *Financial Times*

IN A DARK DARK HOUSE

"Refreshingly reminds us . . . that [LaBute's] talents go beyond glibly vicious storytelling and extend into thoughtful analyses of a world rotten with original sin."   —**Ben Brantley**, *The New York Times*

"LaBute takes us to shadowy places we don't like to talk about, sometimes even to think about . . ."   —**Erin McClam**, *Newsday*

WRECKS

"Superb and subversive . . . A masterly attempt to shed light on the ways in which we manufacture our own darkness. It offers us the kind of illumination that Tom Stoppard has called 'what's left of God's purpose when you take away God.'"   —**John Lahr**, *The New Yorker*

"A tasty morsel of a play . . . The profound empathy that has always informed LaBute's work, even at its most stringent, is expressed more directly and urgently than ever here."   —**Elysa Gardner**, *USA Today*

"*Wrecks* is bound to be identified by its shock value. But it must also be cherished for the moment-by-moment pleasure of its masterly portraiture. There is not an extraneous syllable in LaBute's enormously moving love story."

—**Linda Winer**, *Newsday*

FAT PIG

"The most emotionally engaging and unsettling of Mr. LaBute's plays since *bash* . . . A serious step forward for a playwright who has always been most comfortable with judgmental distance."
—**Ben Brantley**, *The New York Times*

"One of Neil LaBute's subtler efforts . . . Demonstrates a warmth and compassion for its characters missing in many of LaBute's previous works [and] balances black humor and social commentary in a . . . beautifully written, hilarious . . . dissection of how societal pressures affect relationships [that] is astute and up-to-the-minute relevant."
—**Frank Scheck**, *New York Post*

THE DISTANCE FROM HERE

"LaBute gets inside the emptiness of American culture, the masquerade, and the evil of neglect. *The Distance From Here*, it seems to me, is a new title to be added to the short list of important contemporary plays."
—**John Lahr**, *The New Yorker*

THE MERCY SEAT

"Though set in the cold, gray light of morning in a downtown loft with inescapable views of the vacuum left by the twin towers, *The Mercy Seat* really occurs in one of those feverish nights of the soul in which men and women lock in vicious sexual combat, as in Strindberg's *Dance of Death* and Edward Albee's *Who's Afraid of Virginia Woolf*."
—**Ben Brantley**, *The New York Times*

"A powerful drama . . . LaBute shows a true master's hand in gliding us amid the shoals and reefs of a mined relationship."
—**Donald Lyons**, *New York Post*

THE SHAPE OF THINGS

"LaBute . . . continues to probe the fascinating dark side of individualism . . . [His] great gift is to live in and to chronicle that murky area of not-knowing, which mankind spends much of its waking life denying." —**John Lahr**, *The New Yorker*

"LaBute is the first dramatist since David Mamet and Sam Shepard—since Edward Albee, actually—to mix sympathy and savagery, pathos and power."
—**Donald Lyons**, *New York Post*

"*Shape* . . . is LaBute's thesis on extreme feminine wiles, as well as a disquisition on how far an artist . . . can go in the name of art . . . Like a chiropractor of the soul, LaBute is looking for realignment, listening for a crack." —**John Istel**, *Elle*

BASH

"The three stories in *bash* are correspondingly all, in different ways, about the power instinct, about the animalistic urge for control. In rendering these narratives, Mr. LaBute shows not only a merciless ear for contemporary speech but also a poet's sense of recurring, slyly graduated imagery . . . darkly engrossing."
—**Ben Brantley**, *The New York Times*

NEIL LABUTE is an award-winning playwright, filmmaker, and screen-writer. His plays include: *bash*, *The Shape of Things*, *The Distance From Here*, *The Mercy Seat*, *Fat Pig* (Olivier Award nominated for Best Comedy), *Some Girl(s)*, *Reasons to be Pretty* (Tony Award nominated for Best Play), *In a Forest, Dark and Deep*, a new adaptation of *Miss Julie*, and *Reasons to be Happy.* He is also the author of *Seconds of Pleasure*, a collection of short fiction, and a 2013 recipient of a Literature Award from the American Academy of Arts and Letters.

Neil LaBute's film and television work includes *In the Company of Men* (New York Critics' Circle Award for Best First Feature and the Filmmaker Trophy at the Sundance Film Festival), *Your Friends and Neighbors*, *Nurse Betty*, *Possession*, *The Shape of Things*, *Lakeview Terrace*, *Death at a Funeral*, *Some Velvet Morning*, *Ten x Ten*, *Dirty Week-end*, *Full Circle,* and *Billy & Billie.*

EXHIBIT 'A'

SHORT PLAYS & MONOLOGUES BY
NEIL LABUTE

OVERLOOK DUCKWORTH
NEW YORK · LONDON

This edition first published in the United States in 2015 by
Overlook Duckworth, Peter Mayer Publishers, Inc.

NEW YORK:
141 Wooster Street
New York, NY 10012
www.overlookpress.com
For bulk and special sales, please contact sales@overlookpress.com,
or write to us at the address above.

LONDON:
30 Calvin Street
London E1 6NW
info@duckworth-publishers.co.uk
www.duckworth.co.uk
For bulk and special sales, please contact sales@duckworth-publishers.co.uk,
or write to us at the address above.

Cataloging-in-Publication Data is available from the Library of Congress

Book design and type formatting by Bernard Schleifer
Manufactured in the United States of America
ISBN 978-1-4683-1319-2 (US)
ISBN 978-0-7156-5093-6 (UK)
1 3 5 7 9 10 8 6 4 2

for emma sulkowicz and paul nungesser

"people change and forget to tell each other . . ."

—lillian hellman

PREFACE

Let's call this collection "the wild bunch."

The bastard's dozen (in folklore a dozen that is missing one) that makes up this collection is a motley crew at best—not unlike Sam Peckinpah's band of doomed outlaws made famous in his 1969 bloodbath of a film. These eleven plays and monologues have been a part of my life for a few years now—most of them, anyway—and have been waiting for a literary home. The works in this short stack you have before you have all come from a variety of strange little foster homes called "one-act festivals" or theatrical partnerships like AdA (an international collaboration between myself and the Italian playwright/director Marco Calvani) or the like. They were usually given quick births since these kinds of opportunities often spring up at the last moment or with hardly any time to prepare, but I suppose that's part of what makes them such tough little rascals to begin with.

I am proud of these runts—many have been written to fit a theme like "desire" or "censorship" or that kind of thing, or with the directive to create "terror" in the minds and hearts of the audience. A lot of times this has been fun to do since I'm not really someone who tends to be a thematic writer when left to my own devices. That's not to say that a theme (or more than one) doesn't usually find its way into my work along the way, but I rarely (if ever) set out to write a play based on a thematic impulse. I don't write about "race" but instead write about a mixed-race marriage that begins to have troubles. Therefore, to be given a theme ahead of time or a mission such as "scare the shit out of the audience" is like a mini-vacation for a writer who doesn't think that way. That said, it's not always easy. The short form is a real bitch (and don't threaten me with that old "sexist" label again—you know as well as I do that boys can be bitches, too). It's such a blast when you get it right and people always think it's easy to write a few pages and make them great—any time someone does something well it makes the casual onlooker believe that the act itself is easy—but I'm here to tell you that this is just not the case. Like all my other writing, it's hard work but you just have to get in there and get it done. There's no shortcuts and no magic tricks, no little elves who come at night and do the deed for you. When you're a writer, you write. You don't talk about it, you write. Let the writing speak for itself and don't explain it anywhere but on the page.

Writers write. Talkers talk. It's that simple.

10K is the most recent piece in the collection. It was written for the "Summer Shorts" program that is under the direction of J.J. Kandel, whom I've been lucky to work with for the past seven seasons. He's a tireless producer and actor who has brought two of my characters in *Exhibit 'A'* to life (the "Man" in *10K* and the other was in the short play *Here We Go Round the Mulberry Bush* in its New York premiere) along with a spurned young lover in a previous play of mine called *The Furies*. I got the chance to direct *10K* as well, with J.J. and Clea Alsip (a terrific young actress) and we had a great time bringing the main action of the play to life. It's really fun to watch an act as realistic as "running" become so theatrical on the stage; by the time we were in performance both actors sounded more like athletes than actors as they nursed their aching legs each night. *Here We Go Round the Mulberry Bush* was exactly the opposite situation—two actors sat on benches for most of the performance and held an increasingly tense conversation about children and abuse. I was lucky enough to have one of the best stage actors in New York working on yet another play of mine and facing J.J. again (they worked together on *The Furies*): Victor Slezak. I can't say enough about the work of Mr. Slezak. A paragraph wouldn't do it. A book wouldn't be enough. Suffice it to say that he has breathed life into both men and monsters for me, and he's made them beautiful and horrifying in equal measure; he makes each character he plays *matter* and that's all you can ever ask of any actor.

The pieces included here that were part of the AdA project—*I'm Going To Stop Pretending (That I Didn't Break Your Heart)* and *Happy Hour*—had a very lively route to the stage. This edition of AdA (2014) was the second go-round for Mr. Calvani and me. It's a project in which we each write new texts and then direct each other's work. We started the project in Venice this time around, at their Theater Biennale, and that's where an Italian cast worked on my *I'm Going To Stop Pretending (That I Didn't Break Your Heart)* and presented a workshopped staging of it. When it was time to bring the AdA project to New York at the La MaMa facilities, however, we opted to perform a different play instead. This was *Happy Hour*, a new and revitalized version of an earlier play of mine called *A Guy Walks Into a Bar*. I've added new material to it and got the ending right this time around. Marco was blessed with the real-life couple of Jennifer Mudge and Chris Henry Coffey as performers and the audience was lucky enough to watch two peerless actors make dramatic love on stage, night after night.

The Unimaginable and *Some White Chick* were plays written for a shorts fest in London that carried the sobering moniker of "TERROR!" For two years running I was asked to try and really frighten an audience and these two plays were the best I could do. I wanted to create everyday fiends, not some slobbering ghouls or things that go bump in the night. I'm not afraid of vampires and werewolves—I fear the people around me who steal children or find pleasure in the pain and suffering of others. These two little playlets are the results of my fears as a man and a father and a person living in a beautiful world that is peopled with folks that I want to trust but who can't always be trusted. Hey, read the papers—any day's headlines will put my little ghost stories to shame.

The titular play was an invitation to respond to specific bits of censorship that were going on in the U.S. and abroad. *Exhibit 'A'* is an obvious nod to the ill-fated "Exhibit B" art project that was kept from being exhibited in London. I wrote this piece for a group called Theatre Uncut, whom I've worked with several times before and, more specifically, for the theater director Cressida Brown. I was trying to push the limits of this formal exercise—what a surprise!—and show the audience how complicit it can be in an act of abuse as long as someone makes sure to call it "art." I wanted to put the artist under the microscope as much as those who censor and ask one simple question: "Is everything 'art' as long as somebody calls it that?" I certainly have an opinion on the subject and I imagine anyone reading this does as well. That's what makes the subject so damn fascinating, I suppose. "Art." Just ask Emma Sulkowicz and Paul Nungesser for their repective definitions of "art" sometime and you'll see what I mean.

The other pieces that are collected here are a variety of monologues and/or shorter plays that were part of larger benefit performances (*Black Girls, Totally* and *16 Pounds*) or started out as the script for a short film (*BFF*). Each was given life by wonderful actors and directors and exists in that rarified air that is the short dramatic or comedic work—it is a lovely and exclusive club and I'm always glad when I'm asked to be a part of it.

Exhibit 'A' felt like an apt title for the entire collection since everything we do as theater artists is routinely placed under the public microscope and duly examined like evidence in a trial. We are watched and judged and criticized or applauded in the same way that other workers punch the time clock: it's just a part of our lives.

We who do theater do it because we cannot live without it. We simply can't do anything else and even if we could, we wouldn't want to. It is not a matter of choice; it is a matter of necessity. It is everything to us. Theater is both a blessing and a curse and the longest and greatest love affair of most of our lives.

I wouldn't have missed it for the world, even if—*spoiler alert*— I do die in the end, just like Peckinpah's notorious bank robbers before me. Bad news is: it probably won't be in a hail of gunfire by Federales but something lame like high cholesterol or heart disease. Oh well, it's not everyone who gets to die in glorious slow motion and spurting gallons of ketchup . . .

I hope anyone still reading this finds some pleasure buried inside these pages. Know that I did my best writing these plays. Even when they're not perfect, be assured that I tried my hardest each time out.

On a bad day, they suck a little. On a good day, they hardly suck at all (and are, in fact, pretty okay).

May you be reading this on a very good day indeed.

Neil LaBute
November 2015

CONTENTS

10K

10K had its world premiere at 59E59 Theatre as part of the "Summer Shorts" play festival series in New York City in July 2015.
It was directed by Neil LaBute.

MAN   J.J. Kandel
WOMAN   Clea Alsip

A slash (/) indicates the point of interruption between the present line and the next speaker's line.

Silence. Darkness.

A stretch of green. Rolling fields with trees in the distance. A path leading off and over the horizon.

A WOMAN *stands before us, dressed in work-out clothes and stretching.*

She looks very athletic and wears form-fitting clothes. Fancy shoes. She does a fairly complex warm-up routine.

After a moment, a MAN *shows up, starts doing the same thing on the opposite side of the grass.*

Dressed in regular work-out clothes. He does a couple stretches and a few arm swings. That's about it.

For a long moment it's just these two people out there in the tall grass. Warming up for a nice, long run.

After a bit, the WOMAN *glances over and speaks:*

WOMAN   . . . *so* nice out today. Right?

The MAN *smiles and nods. Looks around. Up at the sky.*

MAN   Gorgeous.

WOMAN   No kidding.

MAN   And *no* humidity!

WOMAN   I know!

Silence as they keep warming up. The sun smiling down.

MAN   That's lucky. Right? I mean . . . this part of the country? We're pretty lucky.

WOMAN Uh-huh.

MAN For this time of year . . .

WOMAN Exactly.

A bit more stretching. Another thoughtful comment.

MAN Later in the season.

WOMAN Yep.

MAN August.

WOMAN Right.

MAN Kids back to school soon . . .

WOMAN Not me.

MAN No?

WOMAN Nope.

MAN Oh. (*Points to ring finger.*) But . . . you are . . .?

WOMAN Yes. And I have one. That's two. (*Beat.*) Wait! (*Beat.*) Ha!
I mean *one* child. Just turned *two*.

MAN Got it! So . . . they're always . . .?

WOMAN Yep. Right there. *She* is always right there. Underfoot.

MAN Ha! I remember it well . . .

WOMAN I'll bet.

MAN Oh yeah!

WOMAN You? (*Beat.*) Girls, or . . .?

MAN Boys. *Two*. Great kids, but . . . you know. (*Mimes going crazy.*)
Into everything . . .

WOMAN *Boys.*

MAN Yep.

WOMAN My husband wanted boys . . .

MAN We all do! Husbands. We think so, anyway . . . until we've got
'em . . .

WOMAN True.

MAN Yeah . . . then one trip to the *mall* cures you of *that* stupid idea . . .

WOMAN Ha! (*Pointing.*) Well . . . I should probably get . . . going . . .

MAN Ok. (*Beat.*) You want some company . . . or . . .?

WOMAN Oh. (*Thinking.*) Sure. Ummmmmm . . .

MAN Great.

They nod to each other and then start to "run" (in place) along the path that winds away in front of them.

There they are: running along together now and each lost in their own thoughts.

Jog, jog, jog.

MAN Seriously. Two boys in a *toy store* and all bets are off. (*Beat.*) I think the Chinese are actually on to something . . .

WOMAN Ha! Wait . . . they . . . like boys, don't they?

MAN Oh . . . ummmmmmm . . . I'm not sure. Do they?

WOMAN I think . . .

MAN I thought they didn't like anybody . . .

WOMAN Ha! No, I think that's the *Koreans*.

The MAN *laughs at this and smiles. Points at her.*

MAN Yes! Exactly! My mistake . . .

WOMAN No problem. Or . . . at least *North* Koreans.

MAN Right! I knew it was *some*body Asian!

WOMAN It's the girls they don't want. (*Beat.*) The Chinese, I mean . . .

MAN Oh, yeah . . . I think you might be right about that . . .

WOMAN It's something along those lines. They give 'em away or whatever. Or kill 'em.

MAN . . . *no* . . .

WOMAN I'm not sure. (*Beat.*) Do they throw 'em in the river or am I completely making that up?

MAN Oh, geez, I dunno . . . that's . . . ummmmmmm . . .

WOMAN I think so. They toss 'em right in the river. Don't they? That one major . . . The Yellow River or whatever.

MAN Wait, *what*? No!/ You can't say that . . .

WOMAN Sorry?/ What?

MAN I just . . . the "Yellow" River? *Really*?

WOMAN *What*?

MAN Isn't that just a wee bit . . . you know . . . racist? Or something?/ China? "Yellow" River . . .?

WOMAN No!/ No, that's . . .

MAN . . . ahhhhhhh . . . kinda . . .

WOMAN I mean, I didn't make that up—not just filling in the blank with any old word—that's a *real* place. The *Yellow* River.

MAN Oh.

WOMAN Just like the, ummmmmm . . . the other one . . . the bigger one . . . The Yangtzee. That's the main one. In China.

MAN Oh, sure. Yeah. I've heard of that one.

WOMAN 'Course. (*Beat.*) But the "Yellow's" a river there, too. Just so you know . . .

MAN Okay. Cool./ Didn't know that . . .

WOMAN It's true./ Seriously, though . . . they might actually do that . . . throw their girl babies right *in* the . . .

MAN They *kill* 'em? *Really*? That's . . .

WOMAN Or they used to or something—in ancient times—I feel like I've read that but I could be . . . I'm not sure now. (*Beat.*) But I do know there are *lots* of Asian babies that get adopted and I think they're mostly girls.

MAN Now that *is* true . . . I mean . . . when you see one, or hear about it—or Angelina *buys* another one—it's usually the girl babies coming over here . . . right?

WOMAN Mostly. (*Beat.*) The unwanted ones.

MAN Huh. (*Beat.*) That's wild.

WOMAN But . . . yeah, anyway . . . mine's great. We're *not* throwing her away! (*Beat.*) Giselle.

MAN Ha! Tom Brady must be very proud . . .

WOMAN God! (*Beat.*) Is it *that* obvious?

MAN Kinda.

The MAN *smiles at her as they jog along. She smiles in return. Thinking before she says:*

WOMAN I thought so! (*Beat.*) I told my husband it would be but he didn't listen . . . oh well. She really is beautiful, though . . . so . . .

MAN Great.

WOMAN And so lovely. *So* sweet.

MAN Lucky you. (*Beat.*) I don't mean that my boys aren't that . . . aren't "nice" or whatnot, because they're terrific, they are . . . I just meant in general. You know? (*Beat.*) Boys can be a *real* . . . workout . . .

WOMAN I bet.

They run in silence for a moment. Jogging away down the path. She checks her Fitbit as he wipes away sweat.

WOMAN It's warming up . . .

MAN Sure is. (*Beat.*) I try and get out here in the mornings . . . before it's too hot—well, at least during the summer. Rest of the year I usually go about noon or so . . . I mean, give or take . . .

WOMAN Me, too.

MAN Uh-huh. I feel like I've seen you here before . . .

WOMAN Yeah? (*Beat.*) You look familiar, too . . .

MAN Thanks.

WOMAN Oh. Okay. That wasn't really . . . I mean . . . that wasn't a *compliment* or anything.

MAN *True*! Ha! (*Laughs*.) Sorry!

WOMAN No, I just mean . . .

MAN No, you're right . . . I'm sorry!

WOMAN It *is* nice to see a familiar face . . . even if it's one you don't really know . . .

MAN I get what you mean.

WOMAN Feels a little bit safer . . . out here in the woods and all that. Off the beaten . . .

WOMAN Right. (*Pointing*.) It's a great place to run, though . . . isn't it? Overall, I mean?

WOMAN The game preserve?

MAN Yeah.

WOMAN *Amazing*! All these trails and stuff . . . or around by the pond and then up through . . . totally. I just totally love it out here. (*Beat*.) *So* great . . .

MAN Me, too.

WOMAN Uh-huh.

MAN My wife hates it.

WOMAN Yeah?

MAN Ummm-hmmm. "Nature."

WOMAN She hates *nature*?

MAN Well, it's on her list, anyway . . .

WOMAN Ha!

The MAN *doesn't say anything for a beat or two. Then:*

MAN Her hatred of things does not actually end at "nature" but it is definitely included on her rather *voluminous* list of stuff that she . . . quietly despises . . .

WOMAN Wow.

MAN Yep.

WOMAN That . . . sounds . . .

MAN It is.

WOMAN Yeah?

MAN Yes. (*Beat.*) *Intense.* (*Beat.*) Very.

WOMAN Sorry.

MAN No worries. It's just my . . . *thing* . . .

They run again together for a bit in silence. The MAN *then taps the* WOMAN *on the shoulder.*

He signals that he is about to stop. She stops as well.

WOMAN You okay?

MAN Yeah, I just . . . feels like I've got a rock or something . . . in my shoe . . .

WOMAN Oh. Alright.

MAN I'm gonna . . . I didn't mean for you to . . . you can go on if you want to . . . if you need to be . . ./ I just have to get this whatever-it-is outta my . . . you know?

WOMAN No. Cool. Go for it./ Sure.

MAN Great. Thanks.

WOMAN No problem.

MAN Thanks for that. For waiting.

WOMAN Happy to. (*Beat.*) Nice to run with someone . . .

MAN Agreed.

WOMAN My husband and I used to—before we had the baby and all that, but—plus he's switched jobs now and so he's . . . all . . .

MAN What?

WOMAN He travels sometimes. (*Beat.*) A *lot.*

MAN Got it.

The MAN *reaches inside his shoe and produces a small rock in his hand. He studies it.*

MAN One of the drawbacks of off-roading . . .

WOMAN My *husband*?

MAN No! (*Holding up pebble.*) *This*!

WOMAN Right! (*Smiles.*) Your wife would probably hate that . . . right?

MAN *Yeah*! Gravel in her shoe? That'd be . . . yep. Like the *universe* had singled her out for complete humiliation. (*He throws it away.*) That'd ruin her whole day . . . one little *pebble*.

The guy smiles as he puts his shoe on. Ties it. Stands.

WOMAN Alright. You good?

MAN Absolutely. Let's do it . . .

They nod at each other and take off running. Quiet for a bit while they get back into the rhythm of their pace.

WOMAN How far?

MAN 'Scuse me?

WOMAN How far do you usually go? Out and back, I mean . . .?

MAN Oh. I see. (*Thinking.*) I guess about six miles or so . . .

WOMAN Yeah?

MAN Uh-huh. Takes around an hour.

WOMAN Right. (*Beat.*) Which is about 10K, right?/ I'm the same. I'm only doing five today—right now, I mean—I've got a meeting this morning . . . well, not a "meeting" but a hearing . . . it's . . . nothing. This "thing" so I'm just doing five right now.

MAN Ummmmmmmmmmm . . . I think so. Not sure./ Got it. You're doing a 5K but usually you do the full ten.

WOMAN Yeah.

MAN That was something I just never caught up with in school. (*Gestures.*) All . . . *that* . . .

WOMAN What? Metrics?

MAN Yep! I was the worst . . . so bad at all that shit! (*Beat.*) Sorry, didn't mean to swear.

WOMAN That's totally okay.

MAN I know, and thanks, but I didn't mean to. (*Beat.*) But yeah . . . after, like, the sixth grade I was dead in the water. Math was just . . . like . . . (*Mimes his head exploding.*) BOOM!

WOMAN I was always pretty good at math . . .

MAN That right? Good for you! (*Beat.*) I can remember telling people—even some of my *teachers*—that I was never gonna use any of that stuff again. Algebra? *Calculus*? Or even geometry . . .

WOMAN You told your *teachers* that?

MAN I did! I was kind of a big mouth back in those days . . . (*Laughs.*) And I was *right*!! (*To her.*) You ever needed to know what the volume of a *parallelogram* is? Hmmmmmm? Or a, a, a . . . *cone*?

WOMAN . . . ummmmmmmmmmmmmmmmmmmm . . .

MAN Exactly! (*Beat.*) Volume of an "ice cream cone," maybe, but that's about it! And the volume of an ice cream cone is *full*. That's how much ice cream should be in a cone. Full. To-the-top. (*Laughs.*) *Right*?

WOMAN Ha! That is *so* true!

MAN I'm just saying . . .

WOMAN No, you're completely right about math. Even though I didn't think it was too bad . . . I've never really used it much. (*Beat.*) As an adult, I mean . . .

MAN My point exactly! *So* many hours wasted in school—when I could've been studying all kinds of other things.

WOMAN Such as?

MAN Oh, you know . . . I just mean in *theory* . . . of course . . . "in theory" there were all sorts of other classes that would've made more sense and better prepared me for life . . .

WOMAN Go ahead. I'll bite.

MAN God, I hope so . . .

WOMAN Ha! (*Swats his arm.*) That was dumb . . .

MAN I *know*! Sorry . . .

WOMAN All good. It was funny, though . . .

MAN Thank you.

WOMAN Anyway . . . (*Beat.*) What other classes?

MAN Like . . . I don't know . . . auto mechanics, for one thing!

WOMAN Good one!

MAN *Right*? Changing oil in cars today . . . they now make it so nuts up under there . . . so, that'd be good . . . ummmmmmmmm . . . cooking . . .

WOMAN We did that.

MAN Yeah?

WOMAN Well, "Home Ec."

MAN Oh, yeah, we had that, too, but . . . you know . . . *guys* don't wanna do that . . . with all the sewing! It sounds so . . . whatever.

WOMAN *Feminine*?/ Ha!

MAN Kind of./ *Girly*.

The WOMAN *laughs and shakes her head. He smiles at this.*

WOMAN Ha! Guys are so funny . . .

MAN Yeah. Look who's talking . . .

WOMAN Oh, I know! Women are, too . . . but . . .

MAN *What*?

WOMAN I don't know . . . you're all so . . .

MAN Hey . . . at least nobody throws *us* in the *river*! So . . .

WOMAN Well, that's . . . don't use my *own* facts against me! That's not fair!!

MAN Ha! Okay, okay . . .

WOMAN But, no . . . you're right . . . women do *lots* of silly crap as well . . . but guys are just . . .

MAN I know! We're weird. (*Beat.*) We're weird and retarded and . . . just . . . yeah. I *know*.

WOMAN Yes. I'll give you that.

MAN You, too, though! Just a different kind of weird.

WOMAN Yep. (*Beat.*) Anyhow . . . what else?

MAN Hmmmmm?

WOMAN Classes!

MAN Oh! Right! (*Thinks.*) Ummmmmmmm . . . some sort of money management . . . people skills . . . a general sense of *morals* and . . . *ethics* . . . if they are, in fact, different things.

WOMAN Ha! They *are* . . . I think. And which would be . . . what?

MAN Right and wrong! Like . . . taking *turns* in line at the *deli* . . . that sort of thing . . .

WOMAN Ha!

MAN Managing "road rage." The *basics*.

WOMAN Perfect!

MAN Sex education . . .

WOMAN Uh-oh. *Now* you've done it . . .

MAN What?

WOMAN Nothing, no . . . just . . . ahhhhhhh . . .

MAN Seriously . . . *what*?

WOMAN I was kidding.

MAN No, go ahead. *What*?

WOMAN You know . . . (*Beat.*) We managed to not talk about *that* subject for about 15 minutes or so . . . a man and a woman together. SEX.

MAN . . . I just meant . . .

WOMAN I get it. I do. It's okay.

MAN Yeah, but . . .

WOMAN It just always seems to come up for us. You know? When the opposite sex spends more than . . . like . . . whatever . . . half an hour around each other . . .

MAN I really wasn't trying to . . . you know./ It wasn't "code." Me saying that.

WOMAN Alright./ *Okay*.

MAN Promise.

WOMAN Fine. I believe you.

They run a bit further in silence. Chugging away down the path in front of them.

WOMAN I mean . . . we barely know each other . . .

MAN True.

WOMAN It was an innocent mention of the subject and so no harm done . . . right?

MAN Pretty much.

WOMAN "Pretty much?"

MAN I mean . . . yes . . .

WOMAN You don't seem completely sure . . .

MAN I think I am. Pretty mostly.

WOMAN Ha! "Pretty mostly." That's a new one! (*Smiling*.) Still . . .

MAN Yeah.

WOMAN So . . . then . . . which was it?

MAN I'm . . . you know what? I'm a little bit *lost* now . . . so . . .

WOMAN That's alright. That's cool.

They slow for a second. The WOMAN *holding up her hand.*

WOMAN Should we steer clear, then? *Or* . . .

MAN Of . . . what?

WOMAN *Please.*

MAN You mean . . . "sex?"

WOMAN I do.

MAN Ummmmmmmmmmmmm . . .

WOMAN Happy to, if that's better . . . or we can . . .

MAN Wait, just . . . wait. Hold up.

Another few feet and they come to a stop. Both of them sucking down air, catching their breath.

MAN So . . . do you *wanna* talk about it with me or not . . .? (*Beat.*)
  I'm getting different signals here . . .

WOMAN I mean . . . just as a topic. If you do.

MAN . . . alright . . .

The MAN *drinks from one of those strange little water bottles that he wears on a belt around his waist.*

He offers the WOMAN *a drink. She shakes her head "No."*

WOMAN Still good for you guys?

MAN What's that?

WOMAN You know.

MAN "Sex," you mean?

WOMAN I do.

MAN Ummmmmmmmmmmmmmmm . . .

WOMAN That's actually an answer you just gave me there. Just so
  you know . . . silence is always an answer.

MAN Ha! (*Beat.*) Is it?

WOMAN Kinda.

MAN Yeah. It probably is . . .

WOMAN It *totally* is.

MAN Well . . . then it is. (*Beat.*) Although I did make a sound.
  "Ummmmmm." I wasn't *silent.*

WOMAN Fair enough.

MAN Let's just say . . . that's pretty much on her "list" as well . . . these days.

WOMAN Ooooohhhh . . . really?

MAN Yep. (*Beat.*) Top *five*, probably.

WOMAN Wow.

MAN And climbing . . .

WOMAN Ha!

MAN So . . . yeah . . . not her number one priority any more. (*Beat.*) SEX./ Or, sex with me, anyway . . .

WOMAN Got it./ Understood.

MAN . . . and you?

WOMAN . . .

MAN Alright then.

The WOMAN *nods at this, then looks up, checking the sun.*

WOMAN Shall we?

MAN You bet. Got a few more "K" to go . . .

WOMAN Yes! "Miles to go before we sleep . . ." (*Smiles.*) Or something like that!

MAN What's that?

WOMAN Oh . . . nothing . . . from a poem. I think.

MAN Cool. (*Laughs.*) Another thing I swore I wouldn't use later in life . . .

WOMAN *Poetry?*

MAN All that shit. Reading . . . English Lit.

WOMAN And look . . . I just proved you wrong!

MAN No, that's not . . . *you* used it. Not me.

WOMAN Okay, that's . . . well, yeah. That's true.

MAN And see? (*Smiles.*) Even *that* poet was smart enough to use miles in his poem and not all that other crap . . . *meters* and shit.

WOMAN Ha!

MAN I'm just saying!

WOMAN "Meters to go before I sleep . . ." (*Smiles.*) You really are funny.

MAN Thank you.

WOMAN I like that . . .

MAN Thanks.

They stand for a long moment, staring at each other. This could go either way with just one more gesture.

WOMAN Anyway . . . (*Beat.*) Come on, let's get going before . . . we . . .

MAN What?

WOMAN Nothing. (*Beat.*) Before it gets too late. (*Beat.*) I'm due back soon . . .

MAN Right. (*Beat.*) Right . . .

They start to run again. Pounding down the path through the woods.

WOMAN This is nice.

MAN Agreed. Totally.

WOMAN You usually go around noon, you say?

MAN Yeah . . . a lot of the time. (*Beat.*) I'm self-employed so I've got a little bit of . . .

WOMAN Leeway?

MAN Yeah. Free during the day. If I need to be . . . (*Beat.*) Within reason.

WOMAN That's nice. (*Beat.*) Being your own boss, I mean . . .

He nods and takes another drink while he's running. After he's done, he offers it to the WOMAN. *She mimes "No." He puts the bottle away on his belt.*

MAN And *you?*

WOMAN I'm . . . ummmmm . . . ok. (*Beat.*) A confession . . .

MAN . . . alright . . .

WOMAN My daughter's at home.

MAN . . . *okay* . . .

WOMAN Sleeping.

MAN Oh. (*Beat.*) You mean . . . *now* . . .?

WOMAN Sort of . . .

MAN Alright. (*Beat.*) Sorry, I'm . . .

WOMAN She's home alone.

MAN Oh.

WOMAN Without me. I do that sometimes . . .

MAN *Really?*

WOMAN Yes. I'll wait until she's asleep and then I go out. Running, usually. (*Beat.*) Occasionally errands or just . . . maybe shopping—not for *me,* but groceries or—but it's usually exercise . . . just for an hour. Or so. No more than that, but . . . yeah. I do that. (*Beat.*) Is that horrible?

MAN . . . *no* . . .

WOMAN Ha! God . . . it sounds like it . . .

MAN I mean . . .

WOMAN You can say it.

MAN No, I just . . . you know . . .

WOMAN Go ahead.

MAN Just . . . technically . . . I don't think that you're supposed to . . . like . . . leave *babies* on their own . . .

WOMAN She's two.

MAN Still.

WOMAN She's a big two. 100th percentile in almost all of those categories . . . but yes. You're right. They advise against it . . . and it's commonly looked down upon.

MAN *Categories*?

WOMAN You know . . . the baby categories . . . the ones they check. Weight and height and, and . . . that sort of stuff . . .

MAN Oh. Right. The "categories . . ." (*Beat.*) So, well . . . that's good . . . she's *big*.

WOMAN Ha! BUT.

MAN Yeah. *But* it's still kinda frowned upon.

WOMAN I get it. (*Beat.*) I know.

MAN I'm not judging you . . .

WOMAN Thank you. (*Beat.*) That's rare . . .

MAN Excuse me?

WOMAN No, not from *you*! I didn't mean . . . in my life. That's what I'm saying. There's a *lot* of judgment going on in my life . . . that's what I meant. Personally.

MAN I see. (*Beat.*) Husband?

WOMAN Him. Mother-in-Law. People at church . . .

MAN Neighbors?

WOMAN Thankfully, *no*! (*Beat.*) We live in a nice little . . . it's quiet. A cul-de-sac, but at one end. Not on a through street.

MAN Great.

WOMAN It's a beautiful house . . .

MAN Sounds like it.

WOMAN (*Pointing.*) It's just . . . right over there . . .

MAN Oh. Yeah?

WOMAN Yes. "Whispering Pines." Do you know it?

MAN Ummmmm . . . sure . . . yeah. The subdivision . . . over there. Right off of Hobart. Right?

WOMAN That's it.

MAN *Great* houses in there.

WOMAN Yes.

MAN That's . . .

WOMAN You're judging me.

MAN No. Not at all. (*Beat.*) *Promise*.

WOMAN Thank you . . .

MAN It's hard . . . I know that it is . . .

WOMAN It's . . . (*Beat.*) I used to bring my baby monitor over here and try to . . . but it's out of range. Sometimes you might get a little something . . . a few beeps or whatnot . . . but mostly nothing. (*Beat.*) I did used to do that. For a while.

MAN Yeah, they're made for . . . you know . . .

WOMAN Right. (*Beat.*) Closer.

MAN Uh-huh. And . . .?

WOMAN Nothing. I just come over here . . . to run. For an hour.

MAN Oh.

WOMAN I'll wait to make sure that she's out and I drive over here and do my stretches . . . and then I hit the trail . . . I can do the whole loop in about an hour . . . and then I go right back home. (*Beat.*) Well. Usually. (*Beat.*) I've only ever come in and she was up twice. And awake. Or crying. (*Beat.*) I mean that . . . just *twice*.

MAN Ok.

WOMAN If you think I'm terrible you can just say so . . .

MAN No, that's . . . I mean . . . who am I to judge you on that? Right?

WOMAN I guess.

MAN Honestly. It's so tough being a parent. (*Beat.*) I've done stuff . . . like . . . I mean, small stuff, obviously, but . . . I've run in the drug store—this was before they put in the drive-thru—and left them in the car for a few minutes. The boys . . . you're not supposed to do that. Right?/ Not on a *hot* day, but still.

WOMAN True./ Right.

MAN Or . . . or . . . at the water park once . . . this was a few years back, but . . . I lost track of one of them. "Ethan." My youngest. I lost sight of him for . . . I turned for a *second*, for just, like, *one* second and . . . BAM! He's gone. This huge crowd. People everywhere and kids all look the same . . . it was total panic. Shit. *Un*real.

WOMAN But . . . everything was okay . . .?

MAN Yeah. Sure. (*Beat.*) *Eventually* . . .

WOMAN Oh no. (*Beat.*) What happened?

MAN You know. The routine. (*Beat.*) Calling in security . . . and the P.A. announcements . . . all of that stuff . . . my wife just, like, shooting *daggers* into my back the whole time . . . (*Beat.*) I don't think she's ever really forgiven me for that . . .

WOMAN Oh . . . God . . .

MAN Yeah. (*Beat.*) So . . . yeah . . . I get it . . . your coming over here. For this. (*Beat.*) End of story: Ethan went to the bathroom. Alone. Half-hour of me shitting myself in public but Ethan? He was fine. Toilet paper hanging off his *flip-flops* and this big smile on his face . . . like nothing happened. (*Beat.*) And nothing *did* happen . . .

As they jog he reaches a hand out to her. She takes it and squeezes it. They glance at each other. A smile.

She lets go of his hand and they turn back to their work-out. Both sweating now and burning up ground.

MAN *SO* . . . you can't bring her with you . . . or no family available, or . . . you know, like . . . a sitter . . . or anything? For your work-outs, I'm saying . . .

WOMAN Not that I've been able to . . . my husband is a bit of a . . . I don't wanna say it . . .

MAN No, I get it.

WOMAN Doesn't want just *any*-body touching our child.

MAN Got it.

WOMAN And we're both not local, so . . . there's no family or . . . you know . . .

MAN Right, but . . . I mean . . . people *need* relief.

WOMAN . . .

MAN You can't be on duty all the time. Without help. With a *child*? (*Beat.*) I'm sorry, but that's . . . you can go crazy doing that.

WOMAN I *know*.

MAN No, but I mean, they've done studies . . . post-partum depression and, and . . . even without that . . . just the *stress* of trying to be a good parent . . . and no *sleep* . . . it's seriously dangerous . . . (*Beat.*) Seriously.

WOMAN Thank you.

MAN I'm not being nice here. Really. I'm not.

WOMAN Well, it sure seems like it . . .

MAN Not for you, that's what I'm saying . . . I'm not just saying this for you. To make you feel good. (*Beat.*) It's the *truth*.

WOMAN I appreciate that . . .

MAN Sure. (*Beat.*) I don't think leaving your little—Giselle—leaving her alone, that maybe isn't the answer . . . *but* . . .

WOMAN Right.

MAN You need help. Plain and simple. (*Beat.*) Not *mental*, I don't mean that . . .

WOMAN . . . I probably do, though . . .

MAN Maybe, but right now you need a person. A real, *live* person to help you . . . give you some assistance . . . *support* . . .

WOMAN I dream about that sometimes . . .

MAN Yeah?

WOMAN That kind of thing. A "helper."

MAN I can see why.

WOMAN Not a "helper," per se, but, like . . . a plumber.

MAN A *plumber?*

WOMAN You know . . . from the porno films?

MAN I'm . . . are you kidding? Right now?

WOMAN Yes! Of *course* I am!

MAN Oh.

WOMAN But I do think about someone who just . . . a different *life,*
    I guess . . .

MAN Huh.

WOMAN I guess I don't actually think that much about my daughter
    when I'm dreaming about it, so . . . that's not very . . .

MAN No?

WOMAN *No.* So it's actually more of a new life. Kind of. Thing. (*Beat.*)
    I think more about someone—it's a man, usually—some man who
    actually loves me. Loves me in a way that's *so* obvious and pure
    . . . someone who wants to be around me . . . would do anything
    for me . . . laughs at my jokes and stuff . . . (*Beat.*) Just . . . stupid
    shit like that.

MAN That's not . . . so . . . you know. Outrageous. To want that.

WOMAN *No?*

MAN I don't think so. At *all.*

Silence for a beat while they continue to jog along.

WOMAN Well . . . it seems pretty far away right now. In my life, anyway.

MAN Yeah. I know. I'm sure.

WOMAN But that's what I think about . . . when I'm alone out here.
    On the trail. Or in *bed.*

MAN A man?

WOMAN Yes.

They run in silence for a moment. The MAN *considering all of this.*

MAN What kind of man is he? (*Beat.*) Is he . . . like . . . a *nice* man?

WOMAN Yes, he is . . .

MAN I figured he would be. (*Beat.*) And kind?

WOMAN *Very* kind. To me, he is . . . and funny. I *love* funny!

MAN I see. And handsome, probably?

WOMAN Yes . . . but not completely . . . not so much that it ruins him, at least . . .

MAN Ahhh. (*Beat.*) *That* kind of handsome.

WOMAN Yes. (*Beat.*) He's rugged. An athlete. A *runner.*

MAN Got it.

WOMAN Not too tall . . .

MAN *No*?

WOMAN No . . . and it doesn't bother him . . . that I'm taller than he is . . .

MAN Nice.

WOMAN In fact, he likes it. Finds it amusing.

MAN *Really*? "Amusing?"

WOMAN Of course. He's not a *surface* person, so it makes sense . . . to him . . .

MAN Uh-huh.

WOMAN He's in shape . . . he *adores* me . . . all that stuff. (*Beat.*) The stuff we dream about.

MAN Who?

WOMAN Women.

MAN Guys, too. (*Beat.*) In a partner, I mean . . . we've *all* got fantasies. (*Beat.*) That's not a crime . . . (*Beat.*) Right?

WOMAN I don't think so. As long as they stay that way . . .

MAN And . . . is that what you're planning to do? Keep 'em that way? (*Beat.*) Your . . .?

WOMAN I am . . . yes . . . for as long as possible . . .

MAN Got it.

WOMAN I'm going to live my life, the life that I chose for myself and *committed* myself to . . . with my daughter and my husband . . .

MAN . . . right . . .

WOMAN But in my head . . . my *mind* . . . I'm gonna live this other life . . . a dream life . . . with the man I mentioned. My help *mate*. My "soul" mate.

MAN I see.

WOMAN Just him. And me. Alone together.

MAN Nice.

WOMAN And we're gonna be so happy . . .

MAN I bet you will be . . .

WOMAN And I'm gonna do everything he asks me to do . . . everything he ever *dreamed* of doing as a person . . . *dreamed* of doing with a woman . . .

MAN . . . wow . . .

WOMAN Everything . . .

MAN Yeah . . .?

WOMAN Yes . . .

MAN *Every*thing?

WOMAN Things I've only yearned for before now.

MAN "Things?"

WOMAN Yes.

MAN THINGS.

WOMAN Yes. And other stuff, too . . .

MAN . . . oh God. "Stuff."

WOMAN Without worry. Without regret. Over and over and over again . . .

MAN . . . you and him . . ./ Him and . . ./ And . . .

WOMAN Yes . . ./ Yes . . ./ Yes. Oh yes.

MAN . . . oh shit . . .

The MAN *turns from her, obviously adjusting himself. His underwear. Fighting an erection or something.*

They stop for a moment while he fixes himself. The WOMAN *waits and stretches. Smiles to herself.*

WOMAN Are you alright?

MAN Yes. Sorry. All good. It's all good here. (*Pointing.*) Cramp . . .

The MAN *gets himself under control. Takes another gulp of water. Holds it out for her.*

She declines and waits for him. Checks her Fitbit.

WOMAN Almost done . . .

MAN Sorry?

WOMAN We're almost there . . . my thingie just lit up. My Fitbit. We have over 6,000 steps and, like . . . twenty-some active minutes, so . . . that's . . .

MAN Is that good?

WOMAN That's pretty good.

MAN Great.

A long moment where they are close to each other. Inching a bit nearer to one another with each word or phrase. Almost kissing.

WOMAN So . . ./ Should we . . .?/ Ok./ What?/ Yeah?/To . . .?/ Right. (*Beat.*) Right . . .

MAN Yeah./ Yes. Let's . . ./ No, you know what?/ We should probably go./ Time to get back now./ To *reality* . . . I guess.

They pull back and start jogging again. Taking in the sun and the out-doors and all the rest of it.

A glance at each other, then back to the trail. Silence.

WOMAN Feels so nice to get out, even for just a little bit . . .

MAN Yeah. It's terrific. Exercise.

WOMAN Yep.

MAN I'm . . . you know . . . trying to do it on a regular basis these days . . . like I said before . . .

WOMAN Right.

MAN When I can.

WOMAN Around noon.

MAN Most times. Or mornings . . . I can usually do mornings, too. (*Beat*.) My wife works four days a week—at a flower shop—so I'm pretty good . . . once the boys are . . .

WOMAN Mornings are good for me, too.

MAN Around this time?

WOMAN Right about this time . . .

MAN Before it gets too hot.

WOMAN Yes.

MAN Yeah.

WOMAN Nice.

MAN Yep.

They slowly come to a stop. Back where they started.

They do a bit more stretching. Walking around and cooling down.
Glancing at each other.

WOMAN Made it! (*Beat*.) Well . . . I better get back.

MAN You should.

WOMAN For . . .

MAN Right. I know. "Giselle."/ Before someone goes and throws her in the river.

WOMAN Right!/ Ha! Anyway . . . it was great talking with you . . . about things . . .

MAN Yes!

WOMAN All *sorts* of things . . .

MAN True.

WOMAN And dreams . . .

MAN Uh-huh.

WOMAN Which was okay, wasn't it . . .? To . . .

MAN Sure . . . absolutely yes . . .

WOMAN I mean . . . dreams can't hurt anything . . . can they?/ (*Beat*.) *Can* they?

MAN Not really . . . I mean . . ./ No.

WOMAN Not if you don't let them . . .

MAN Right. If they just stay that way. (*Beat*.) As, like . . . "dreams."

WOMAN Exactly! No, then they're . . .

MAN They're just "dreams." (*Beat*.) Right?

WOMAN Yes. And nothing more . . .

MAN Exactly.

WOMAN "Dreams."

MAN . . . yeah.

WOMAN As opposed to . . . you know . . .

MAN What?

WOMAN Just . . . real stuff, I guess. *Reality*.

MAN True.

WOMAN Because reality is . . . *so* . . .

MAN Exactly.

WOMAN *So* messy.

MAN Yep.

WOMAN Lies . . . and, and . . . like . . .

MAN Secrets.

WOMAN Definitely secrets!

MAN And . . . lies . . .

WOMAN I said that already.

MAN Right! You did . . . "lies" . . .

WOMAN And secrets . . .

MAN Yes. Which *I* mentioned . . .

WOMAN And plans. Always planning little *trysts.*

MAN I guess.

WOMAN I mean . . . I would *imagine*, anyway . . .

MAN Sure. "Planning." And "trysts."

WOMAN And hurt. *Real* people being hurt . . .

MAN Right. "Hurt." And deceived.

WOMAN Yes . . . or even worse./ Yes. Found out.

MAN *Worse*?/ Right. Exposed.

WOMAN So . . . yes . . . *trust* me. It's probably better to just *dream* about this. All of this./ *All* of it.

MAN . . . maybe so . . ./ Yep.

WOMAN I do. I think so. I *definitely* do. (*Beat.*) Better than secrets . . . and lies . . . and . . . and . . .

MAN . . . hurt . . .

WOMAN Yes. (*Beat.*) "Hurt."

They stare at each other for another long minute. After a second, she holds out her hand. He reaches out to take her hand but she nods "No." Points to his water bottle.

WOMAN I will take a sip, though. If you don't mind.

MAN . . . no . . . that's . . . not at all. *No.*

The MAN *fumbles to get it out again. Holds it out for the* WOMAN.

She takes it and holds it near her mouth but not right up to it. Instead, she squeezes and lets a long, thin stream of water cascade into her mouth.

He stands there. Watching her. Transfixed.

The WOMAN *finishes and hands the bottle over. Wiping her mouth with the back of her hand.*

WOMAN   . . . have a good one./ What, *meters*?

MAN   Yeah, you, too. (*Beat.*) I'm probably gonna go do a few more . . . you know . . ./ Ha! Yeah. "Meters." (*Reciting.*) "Meters to go before I . . ."

WOMAN   Ha! (*Laughs.*) Cool.

MAN   Yep.

WOMAN   See you soon?

MAN   Hope so.

WOMAN   Yes.

MAN   I really do.

WOMAN   Yes.

MAN   I'd like that . . .

WOMAN   Yes. (*Beat.*) Me too . . .

MAN   Good. That's . . . (*Beat.*) Good.

The WOMAN *smiles and turns. Walks off toward the parking lot in the distance.*

The MAN *watches her go. Takes a drink from the bottle and then replaces it.*

He spins in a series of tight circles. Wondering what all of this means to him and his little life.

After a moment, the MAN *turns and runs away, with his eyes staring off into the distance.*

Silence. Darkness.

HERE WE GO ROUND THE MULBERRY BUSH

HERE WE GO ROUND THE MULBERRY BUSH had its world premiere as part of the "LaBute Short Play Festival" at the St. Louis Actor's Studio in St. Louis, MO, in July 2014.
It was directed by Milton Zoth.

KIP Reginald Pierre

BILL William Roth

Silence. Darkness.

A stretch of grass and flower beds. Benches as well. Some corner of a park somewhere. The sound of children playing in the distance.

*A man in his 50s sitting on one of the benches. He has a paper with him but he's not reading it. This is "*BILL*."*

He just sits. And watches. Checks his watch from time to time. Takes a bite from an unwrapped sandwich.

After a moment another man enters. Sits on a bench near BILL*. He's mid-30s. Work clothes. His name is "*KIP*."*

BILL *glances at* KIP*. Nods.* KIP *returns the gesture. They sit. They watch.*

KIP . . . great day, huh?

BILL Gorgeous.

KIP Yeah. I know. (*Beat.*) Terrible winter we had, so . . . thank God. Right?

BILL Uh-huh. So cold.

KIP Yep. That was the thing . . . people saying it was one of the worst on record and all that, but to me it just seemed cold. The snow stuck around because of that . . . not like it just kept coming . . . piling up or anything . . . but really cold. So it stayed.

BILL That's true.

KIP Anyway . . . (*Pointing.*) It's spring now. It feels great—last few weeks, month even—it's been fantastic.

BILL I agree.

KIP And perfect over here. In the park.

BILL Oh yes. This is *such* a nice spot.

KIP Yeah?

BILL Mmmmmmm. On a day like this? Wonderful. (*Beat.*) I'll sit here for hours when I'm not working. Taking in the sun.

KIP I'll bet.

BILL Quiet, you know? More so than the rest of the park. Down by the ball fields. Other places like that. And gorgeous light . . .

KIP Right.

BILL A bit more secluded.

KIP Yeah, I can see that . . .

BILL You can read, or . . . you know . . . have your lunch. (*Indicates.*) A sandwich.

KIP Uh-huh. (*Beat.*) Yeah, it's tucked back in here a ways. Off the path. That's nice. (*Waits.*) Listen to those kids . . .

BILL I know.

KIP So happy to be outta the house . . . makes you smile to hear 'em out there, laughing and playing. Doesn't it?

BILL Yes. (*Listens.*) Sounds like they're having fun . . .

KIP Totally. (*Beat.*) That doesn't bother you?

BILL Excuse me?

KIP No, I just mean . . . when you were saying it stays quieter over here—this end of the park—that doesn't bug you? The kids? If you're reading your paper or whatever . . . eating your sandwich?

BILL No. Not at all.

KIP Well, that's good . . .

BILL Yes, they're fine. (*Pointing.*) They're *way* over there. Down by the—pretty far away.

KIP Oh. Right. Yeah, I see . . . by that little gate. (*Beat.*) Some probably come up this way, though, right? A few?

BILL Sometimes. Not too often.

KIP Huh.

BILL No, they're not much of a bother. (*Beat.*) They just like to explore and that sort of thing. Bring their dogs up here . . .

KIP Nice. (*Beat.*) You got any?

BILL Animals?

KIP No! The other kind . . .

BILL Hmmmm?

KIP *Kids.* Do you have children?

BILL Oh! Sorry! (*Laughs.*) I don't. No. None of my own . . .

KIP Got it.

BILL Wasn't lucky enough for that to happen in my life . . . *so* . . .

KIP Huh. But you'd like some? Or one, even? I mean . . . if you could?

BILL Ummmmmm . . .

KIP You don't have to answer that! Sorry.

BILL That's alright.

KIP None of my business, really . . .

BILL It's fine.

KIP I mean . . . not "none" but you don't have to say anything. (*Beat.*) If you don't wanna.

BILL What's that?

KIP What?

BILL I didn't follow you . . .

KIP About . . .?

BILL You said something . . . I missed the part about . . . did you say that it was or was not your business? My having children? (*Beat.*) Sorry?

KIP Ummmmmmmm . . . neither. I said it was sort of somewhere in-between, I guess.

BILL I'm not . . . I'm afraid I'm lost . . . *what*?

KIP In-between.

BILL What does that mean?

KIP I mean . . . yes . . . you're right . . . it's not really my "business" if you have a kid or not, that's not what I'm—but *I* have a kid, and you know him. And that is my business. (*Beat.*) That part. (*Beat.*) They won't be coming here today, by the way. My wife. My kid. (*Beat.*) Today it's just gonna be me. (*Beat.*) You and me.

BILL . . .

KIP (*Looking over.*) Well, that made you quiet.

BILL No . . . not at all . . . I just don't . . .

KIP *What*? (*Beat.*) Don't know what to say . . . or which one I'm talking about? Which kid?

BILL I don't . . . I'm not sure I like your tone. Mr. . . .?

KIP Simms. My name is "Kip Simms." Yours?

BILL I'm "Bill." (*Beat.*) My name's "Bill."

KIP Oh. (*Waits.*) "Bill" what?

BILL "Bill Jensen."

KIP "Bill Jensen." (*Beat.*) Yeah, you're him. I got the right guy. (*Beat.*) I suppose there was always the chance that I could've sat down next to someone else . . . different guy who accidentally sat where you usually do in the afternoons . . . that is *possible*.

BILL Listen . . . Mr. Simms . . . I'm not sure . . .

KIP "Kip" really is fine, you can just call me that. "Kip." I prefer it.

BILL Fine, "Kip" . . .

KIP No need to get formal or anything.

BILL . . . alright . . .

KIP Not yet, anyway . . .

Silence for a moment. KIP *keeps looking into the distance as* BILL *looks over at him. Studying him.*

KIP You don't know me. Haven't seen me before or anything . . . it's not that.

BILL I didn't think so.

KIP Doesn't matter how long you look at me or search your memory

. . .

BILL Look, what's this about? Honestly?

KIP It's about you.

BILL Me?

KIP Yeah. About you . . . and my son.

BILL *looks over at* KIP *and blanches at this. In silence.*

BILL (*Checks watch.*) . . . I'm sorry, but my lunch is almost over and
I need to go . . . this is, ummmmmmmmmm . . .

KIP You should probably take a long lunch.

BILL What?

KIP That's *advice*. Not a *threat*.

BILL Yes, but . . . why would I . . .?

KIP Because. You just should.

BILL . . . *look* . . .

KIP Because I have some things to say to you and you need to hear
them or I'm going to tell them to somebody else. Other people.
People that you would probably not at all like me talking to . . .

BILL . . .

KIP Does that make sense? (*Beat.*) *Bill?*

BILL *doesn't respond but sits back on his park bench and waits.* KIP
lets him stew for a moment. Silence.

BILL Yes. I mean . . . yes. I suppose.

KIP Yeah. It does. You know it does.

BILL And who's your son? (*Beat.*) If I may ask?

KIP Sure. You can ask . . . you just did. (*Beat.*) Or maybe you can
guess. (*Beat.*) "Taylor." Taylor is my son. "Taylor Simms."

BILL Oh.

KIP Yeah. You know "Taylor," right? Adorable little guy . . . four years old. Blond. You *know* which one. (*Beat.*) Right, Bill?

BILL Yes . . . I mean . . . there's a boy who comes by here . . . with his *mother* . . . named "Taylor." (*Beat.*) Some afternoons.

KIP That's him.

BILL So, yes. I know him. If that's the one . . .

KIP 'Course it is. You *know* that's the same one. You already know that.

BILL Alright. (*Beat.*) I didn't know his last . . .

KIP Unless there's other boys. On other afternoons. (*Beat.*) If there are, if that's the case, then this is probably a bit confusing right now and if that's true then I'm sorry. (*Beat.*) Sorry about that, Bill.

BILL . . .

KIP He talks about you. Taylor does. (*Beat.*) Isn't that funny? He talks about you at home. When I get back from work. In the evening. After dinner. Sometimes during but mostly after. When I've got time to sit around and play with him at night . . . he talks about you.

BILL . . .

KIP About this man at the park. "Bill."

BILL But . . . that's . . . not . . .

KIP No, it's you. I know it's you that he's talking about. Let's not waste time on that. 'Kay? (*Beat.*) O-kay?

BILL Fine.

KIP Yeah. "Fine."

BILL But . . .

KIP My son talks about the "nice man at the park." (*Beat.*) Which is you, Bill. He is talking about you. (*Beat.*) Is he right?

BILL I'm sorry?

KIP Is-he-right?

BILL I don't know what you're asking me . . .

KIP Are you a nice man? "Bill Jensen?" (*Beat.*) Had to ask my wife your last name . . . she couldn't remember it at first . . . but hey.

BILL . . . this is really *outrageous*, do you know that? (*Beat.*) It is. (*Beat.*) I mean it.

KIP Of course you do.

BILL I do! I mean . . . coming here, and, and . . .

KIP What?

BILL Just . . . talking to me like this!

KIP I haven't really said that much to you.

BILL Ha!

KIP Well, you can laugh and be whatever it is that you're acting like you are, but it's true. I've only said a couple things. And asked you a question . . . (*Beat.*) A question that you didn't answer yet.

BILL What?

KIP Are you "nice?" Is my son right about you or not?

BILL Yes. (*Beat.*) I'm nice.

KIP Okay.

BILL I am.

KIP Fine.

BILL I'm a good person . . .

KIP Let's not get carried away, Bill. All I asked was the "nice" part. "Good" is a *whole* different thing . . .

BILL Alright, well, I need to . . . (*Gathers up his paper.*) . . . I really do have to get to my office now, so . . . you're going to have to excuse me . . .

KIP At "Beneficial," you mean?

BILL *stops in his tracks. Looks over at* KIP. *Silence for a moment.*

BILL What're you doing here? What is this?

KIP That's right, isn't it? Where you work?

BILL   *Yes.*

KIP   I didn't learn that from Taylor. I mean, that would've been *amazing* for a kid his age to know that. Right? To remember it. (*Beat.*) But his mom remembered—you know, "Trish," my wife Trish, whom you're *so* chatty with, apparently, when they come over here during the week and talk with you, on these benches here— Trish could remember that. (*Beat.*) "Beneficial."

BILL   . . .

KIP   One of the few things that you let slip about yourself. Where you work. (*Beat.*) When I asked Trish about you—and I'll be honest, I sorta *grilled* her about you—once I started hearing about you, every day from my son . . . all she could do was give me a sort of general description of you and come up with where you worked . . . at "Beneficial." (*Beat.*) She even defended you, Bill. At *first*. Said some very nice things about you.

BILL *is still standing. He looks off, trying to decide if he should leave or not. He doesn't, though. Instead,* BILL *stays right where he is.*

BILL   You have a lovely family. Trish and your son. (*Beat.*) I mean that. (*Beat.*) I *do*.

KIP   Uh-huh.

BILL   She's very nice to talk with. Your wife.

KIP   That's good.

BILL   And your son . . . he's . . . Taylor's . . .

KIP   I'm gonna stop you right there, Bill. You can stop talking. Right now.

BILL   . . .

KIP   Because, see, I don't really give a shit if you like them or not. Honestly. Could not care less. (*Beat.*) The thing I *do* care about, though, is that you stop. Just go away now . . . stop doing what

you're doing with them. From this moment on. Got it? (*Beat.*)
I want you to disappear.

BILL Listen, I'm not . . .

KIP *BILL.*

BILL What?

KIP Do you *get* it? What I'm saying? I need an answer from you.
Right now.

BILL Yes, but . . . listen . . .

KIP That's all that matters.

BILL No, I'm trying to say something now, so *listen* to me . . .
please . . .

KIP Bill . . . just stop . . .

BILL *No*, I'm going to say something here! You are not going to
railroad me with all of your *tones* and your . . . your *accusations*.
(*Beat.*) I have done nothing wrong here . . . at all. Nothing. (*Beat.*)
I have talked to your wife . . . to Trish . . . that is true, and your son
as well . . . but there has been no wrong-doing of any kind. Of *any*
kind. I didn't seek them out, I haven't . . . Trish speaks to *me,* if
anything, she speaks to me and I'll tell you something, she is a
lonely person. Maybe you don't like hearing that but it's true.
She's lonely and she has sought out my friendship, not the other
way around. Maybe you should speak to her about that at some
point. Alright? About why she comes by in the afternoons.

KIP I see.

BILL And whatever you're implying about your son—about Taylor—
is sickening to me . . . that is just . . . well, you *really* need to look
at your own personal relationships, Mr. Simms. (*Beat.*) I'm sorry to
be blunt like this, I'm not a rude person, but I can't listen to any
more of this without defending myself. (*Stands.*) I think this is
awful, what you've done, but I need to ask you to *please* tell your

wife to leave me alone from now on. To go elsewhere in the park with your son, and I think that's unfortunate but that's the way it goes. Nothing to be done. (*Beat.*) And now I really do need . . . to be . . . I have to . . .

BILL *starts to walk away.* KIP *lets him get pretty far and then calls out to him:*

KIP   Oregon.

BILL *stops in his tracks. Back turned to* KIP. *Stands in silence.*

KIP   I wasn't sure about it—I mean the photo looks like a younger you—but if just the word makes you stop like that . . . *Oregon* . . . then it *must* be you. (*Beat.*) Right?

BILL *turns and looks at* KIP. KIP *sits there, watching him and waiting before he says anything else.*

KIP   I don't know why they don't help you guys change your names when you move from spot to spot. State to state.

BILL   . . .

KIP   I suppose that would defeat the purpose, though. Make it harder to track you from place to place. And that's the point. You need someone to keep an eye on you. Don't you? (*Beat.*) Bill?

BILL   . . .

KIP   Because if not . . . if people just forgive and forget you . . . then you're free to do whatever it is you wanna do. Move from Oregon to here—with a few stops in-between, I imagine—get a job any-where you like, go to the park on your lunchtime . . . (*Beat.*) If folks don't keep track of you then you can pretty much just go around acting like you're a normal guy. A "nice" guy. (*Beat.*) Isn't that right, Bill? Bill Jensen of Eugene, Oregon?

BILL   That isn't me.

KIP No?

BILL No, it isn't.

KIP You're not "Bill Jensen" from Eugene? A guy whom I was able
to track down for about fifty bucks' worth of police records there
on the Internet? (*Beat.*) Hmmmmmmmmm?

BILL No.

KIP It's pretty easy to prove, Bill.

BILL I'm saying I'm not *that* person anymore.

KIP Oh, I *see*. So you're . . . it's more a . . . *philosophical* response
than the truth, is that what it is? Because you are the right guy.
From that place. Who did what you did. (*Beat.*) A few times.

BILL But . . . that's not who I am now.

KIP Ok, well, that's something we could talk about for a long time,
I'm sure—debate that for the rest of the month and we *still* might
not end up agreeing about that little fact . . . but you're the guy.
From that website. And I'm not sure that my wife or my son or
your job would really be able to identify the *subtleties* that you're
referring to. In your character. (*Beat.*) The "new" you.

BILL *looks at* KIP. *A deep sadness settles over his face. Tears in his
eyes, even.* KIP *is unmoved.*

KIP Do you get what I'm saying here? Bill?

BILL I'm a different person today.

KIP Same name, though. If the authorities really felt the same way
that you do . . . you think they'd make it like the, ummm, you know
. . . "Witness Protection Program" or something . . . really help you
disappear into a new identity or whatever. But they don't. Do
they? (*Beat.*) No. They don't . . .

BILL . . .

KIP . . . and I think the reason that is, it's because you haven't really turned over a new leaf . . . gone through some big change and come out the other side a completely new and reformed person . . . I think you've been allowed to move out of their state, that's all. You've been spit outta the system and sent on your merry way to do as you please in some other state. With some other person's kids. Some unsuspecting grandparent or wife or whomever. That is what I think the situation we find ourselves in here is . . . Bill.

BILL You don't know me, Mr. Simms. What I have gone through. What I live with. You don't and you never will.

KIP You're right. I don't because I'm not you or a person like you . . . (*Points.*) I do not hear the sounds of children playing in a park and get turned on.

BILL *starts to say something but* KIP *holds up a hand and stops him.* KIP *continues:*

KIP That's the difference. I'm not sick. Like you. I don't have a disease like yours . . . no matter how much I work or how "lonely" my wife is or the time I have to give up with my son because I'm out of town on business trips . . . whatever shortcomings I have as a person and a man and a dad and a husband . . . I'm still nothing like you. (*Beat.*) Am I? (*Beat.*) Bill Jensen?

BILL No.

KIP Correct answer.

BILL You'll never be like me . . . and you don't know how lucky you are because of that. (*Beat.*) You'll never feel my pain . . . what I carry around inside me.

KIP You know what, Bill? I am unmoved. That's the problem with facts. The cold fucking facts of a person's life. (*Beat.*) I have read what you've done. Just sitting there on a piece of paper that was faxed to me. For anybody to see. Your history. (*Beat.*) And after you sift through a few pages of that . . . a student . . . and a—what was it?—someone's cousin, one side of your family or the other . . . after thumbing through the things you've done . . . no. I can't feel the pain you carry inside. I cannot. I'm too busy thinking of the pain that you have caused in your lifetime. Lots of fucking pain . . . to lots of other people.

BILL *looks at* KIP *and tries to hold his gaze but he can't and turns away.*
BILL *lowers his gaze as he goes over and sits on a different bench.*

KIP I'm sure you're better. Right now. Sure that you're showing *remarkable* restraint these days. That's probably true. (*Beat.*) And so am I. I am restraining myself from moving over there next to you and pulling your *cock* out through your *throat*. That's what I wanna do. To you. But I'm not. No. Because I'm showing remark-able restraint.

KIP *stands up, reaches inside his coat pocket. Produces a small rubber ball. A toy soldier. A little book.*

KIP I stole these from my boy. He loves them. Carries 'em around the house all the time and wants me to read him the book and to play with the ball and the soldier . . . but I'm giving them back to you now. *Here.*

KIP *moves over to* BILL *and puts the items in his hands. Sits next to him.*
KIP *doesn't say anything else. Just sits there, staring off into the distance.*
BILL *glances over at him.*

KIP He's gonna cry tonight . . . later, when he can't find that stuff . . . and when you're not around or they go to some new playground or that sorta thing . . . he's gonna cry. About you. Missing you. I hate doing that to Taylor . . . but he's four and pretty soon, you know what? He'll forget. About you and those toys and everything

else . . . and life—mine and his and Trish's—it'll go on. Happily.
Without you anywhere nearby.

BILL *turns the toys over in his hands. Not looking at* KIP *while he does this.*

BILL   This was my brother's. (*Holds up soldier.*) When he was a little
boy.

KIP   Huh.

BILL   He was older than me . . . my brother . . . and he died when he
was about ten. Back home.

KIP   In Oregon?

BILL   Yes. (*Beat.*) The year we moved there.

KIP   That's too bad. Sorry.

BILL   It's alright. (*Beat.*) He was hit by a car. In our new neighborhood.

KIP   I see.

BILL   And I kept a few of his things . . . all this time, I've held onto
these little relics of his. (*Holds out his hand.*) A few that I gave to
your son and some others still in my possession at home. In my
apartment . . . (*Beat.*) I'm not saying any of this as an excuse or
some kind of . . . as a sort of . . . reason for this, any of this . . . I sit
at this bench most days, a lot of the time since I moved here, to
this city, so I can get away from people, not for a vantage point for
. . . for . . . you know . . . I honestly don't. That's not what I do. I'm
trying to be alone, to live a life where I'm alone and doing good . . .
I said "I'm a good person" to you and I meant that. On the inside.
Inside of me I am and I'm striving to be that. Now. Every day.
(*Beat.*) I didn't ask your wife to be here when I was here. I didn't
want your son to run up the hill one day and sit there . . . on my
bench . . . and to smile over at me and laugh and, and, and
. . . I didn't do anything to make that happen. It's not *fair*. It's not
fair to me. (*Beat.*) What I've done is in the past and it's not fair to

punish me like this. What you are saying to me . . . doing to me here. (*Beat.*) Please. I'm not asking you to understand me or who I am or what I've done . . . but can't you see that it's not right . . . to . . . for you to do this to me now?

KIP No.

BILL "No?"

KIP I hear you, what you've just said . . . but I can't feel that. Inside me. That what I'm telling you is wrong. (*Beat.*) What's wrong is that I'm not gonna tell somebody what you're doing with your afternoons—*that's* wrong. I'm remiss in not letting anyone at your place of work know about who you are and what secrets are hidden away in your past. (*Beat.*) I'm letting you go . . . like the police and the social workers that I condemned before. I'm telling you to go away, to run off and bother some other family or co-worker or innocent child. That's what I'm doing. That is what I'll get to live with and probably pick up the paper one day and see your face there, in a photo, blinking back at me . . . like you are right now . . . with that "what have I done?" look on your fucking face . . . *that* is the mistake I'm about to make . . . but I guess I can live with that.

BILL . . . please . . .

KIP Bill. Don't. (*Beat.*) Trish has no idea that I'm doing this. Obviously neither does Taylor. I don't want their lives changed one iota from what it was since the last day they came here. (*Beat.*) But you will go away. Elsewhere. You will.

BILL And . . . I mean . . . if I didn't? (*Beat.*) What then?

KIP I'll kill you. I'm not joking and I'm not a violent person . . . I didn't grow up in a house like that but I'm gonna come back here . . . this week and a month from now . . . three years . . . doesn't matter. I will be *back*. Occasionally and often. And if I find you here, sitting in the sunlight and reading your paper and listening to

the children playing . . . I will *kill* you. Do you understand me?
Kill you dead.

BILL Yes.

KIP I'm not playing a game. I'm not trying to be funny or clever or make idle threats. (*Beat.*) I am protecting my child. Taylor will never see you again and you . . . there will never ever be a time when you have him on your knee as you read that book to him or you talk to my wife or what ever else you've done . . . so *carefully* . . . so *cautiously* . . . acting like it was the most natural thing in the world to pick him up and laugh and hold him while you gave Trish advice and *gossiped* about all the shows that she loves to watch. (*Beat.*) Here or at your office or in front of a courtroom of people—it doesn't matter to me—I'll kill you. I will *waste* the rest of my life doing that. To you. To destroy you and what you are.

BILL . . .

KIP *stretches and* BILL *flinches at this.* KIP *doesn't do it to intimidate* BILL *but he doesn't hate the result.*

KIP So you decide. Bill. What you want to do next. Think about that while you're here and the sun is warming your face . . . think about if it's worth it or not . . . for you to come back here again. (*Beat.*) Okay?

BILL I've done nothing wrong.

KIP Alright.

BILL I have done *nothing* to your family that is wrong . . . I've . . . I've . . . I've . . .

KIP Fine.

BILL I haven't!

KIP Whatever you say, Bill.

BILL   Your wife talks to *me*!

KIP   Uh-huh.

BILL   She keeps coming here to speak with *me* about things. Not the other way around.

KIP   I hear you.

BILL   Your son ran up the hill . . . from there . . . right over there, the first time. Ran up here to me! Where *I* was already sitting!

KIP   Right.

BILL   He came running to *me*. Up here to *me* and sat on *my* bench. (*Pointing.*) Right there.

BILL *is trying to get through to* KIP *but it doesn't seem to be working.*

Suddenly, KIP *turns and grabs* BILL *by both lapels. Pulls him close. Face to face. Shakes him hard. Once. Twice. Three times.*

Silence as KIP *lets go of* BILL. BILL *slowly collects himself as the moment of restrained violence speaks for itself.*

KIP   I understand. (*Beat.*) And you understand me, too, right? Don't you, Bill? (*Beat.*) You do . . . don't you?

BILL   . . . yes.

KIP   Then good.

KIP *nods and reaches over. Pats* BILL *on the leg, and then gets up.*

KIP   . . . great day, huh? (*Beat.*) Gorgeous.

KIP *moves away and exits.* BILL *sits there, with a handful of toys and his newspaper.*

Suddenly his face reddens. Twisted. Angry. Shamed. Hurt. He has been caught out and he is furious. He bursts into tears. Sobs for a moment. Alone on the bench.

BILL   (*To himself.*) . . . I've done nothing wrong . . . I've done *nothing* wrong here . . . I've done nothing *wrong* . . . I've done nothing . . . wrong . . .

BILL *stomps his feet and wraps his arms around his chest. Trying to comfort himself. Holding back a scream. Tears running down his cheeks.*

BILL (*To himself.*) . . . nothing . . . nothing . . . *nothing* . . .!

He sits there, fighting to regain his composure. Holding himself. Rocking back and forth.

The sound of children playing in the distance. Growing.

Silence. Darkness.

HAPPY HOUR

HAPPY HOUR had its world premiere as part of the AdA "Desire" project at La MaMa in New York City in October 2014.
It was directed by Marco Calvani.

TED   Chris Henry Coffey
CLEO   Jennifer Mudge

Silence. Darkness.

We're in a club of some sort. Loud music. People dancing and drinking and occasionally trying to connect.

*A guy (*TED*) walks in. He stands near a table with a drink. Various other drinks on the table—he's been here for a while. He's coming back from the bar with a fresh drink.*

After a moment, he signals toward somebody. Laughs. Holds up his drink. Does a little dance, pointing toward the unseen person across the room.

Laughs. Does the dance one more time, a little bit more exaggerated this time. Maybe even a spin or two.

He signals to this person that, no, he does want to join him (or her) on the dance floor. Laughs. Waves. He then does a little bow. Waves. Bows again. Okay, that's odd.

TED *looks around some more. checks his watch. Taps a toe while he sips from his drink.*

Apparently his phone is ringing because he begins to feel his jacket searching for his cell. Outside pockets. No luck. Inside pocket on one side. No luck again. Other side is the same result.

Finally checks his pants and there it is. He pulls it out and answers it.

When he starts speaking he does so loudly, over driving music (The sound is there to set the mood but disappears once this begins. The "shouting" is just for effect.)

TED . . . hello? (*Beat.*) Honey? Can you hear me?! What?! Can you . . . you can hear me?! Yes?!! Or no?! No?! I don't know . . . I'm having a bit of trouble hearing you, so I wondered if you can hear me. Can you? Yes? No? (*He waits.*) Honey? I'm saying . . . oh, ok. Great. You can? Good. (*Beat.*) Yeah, it's loud in here. Really loud. No, I don't know the name of the song . . . it's new, I think . . . huh? No, I don't have that on my phone. SIZZLE. *What*? Oh . . . SHAZAM. No . . . I still have a Blackberry.

TED *spots someone across the floor and raises up his drink. Smiles. Signals that he can't come over there right now. Back to his call:*

TED Sorry, what? What?! See, you're going in and out . . . yeah. Uh-huh. No, I don't think I can ask them to turn it down. No. It's a club, sweetie . . . yes. I told you that! I did, too! Yes. These guys like to go out. That's what they do. No, all the time. It is a serious part of their heritage. Ok, no, not that . . . maybe not their heritage, but their . . . you know . . . whatever this is. "Society." No, that's not—the "culture." Yes, it is a big part of their culture. (*Waits.*) What? Oh, you have a call? Ok. That's fine . . . no, take it. I should get back to the . . . what? Honey, what about the call you have coming in? Ok. Ok. Yeah, I will look it up . . . when I get home, I'll have the answer for you. Yeah. It does have a good beat . . . you're right. (*Beat.*) Oh, they're calling again . . . who is it? No, that's alright. Grab it. Yes. I'll call you later. (*Beat.*) No! Not too late! Okay! 'Bye! Yes! 'Bye! Love you! 'Bye!

TED *is exhausted after this. He practically finishes off his drink. Waves at someone else. Taps his toe again.*

*After a moment, a gal (*CLEO*) comes over. Stands near him. She is a certified knock-out.*

TED *glances over. Nods. She nods back and gives him a big smile as well.*

She drinks something sophisticated and sways a little with the beat of the music.

TED *smiles at this. She smiles back but doesn't stop her dancing. He does his little dance for her this time and then laughs at himself.*

CLEO *laughs too, but not at him. With him.* TED *takes one more sip of his drink. Checks his watch. Waits.*

She looks over at him again. TED *moves a little closer to her. Shouts in her direction:*

TED   . . . don't do it! Seriously. Don't. I'm not worth it . . .

CLEO   What's that?

TED   Nothing! (*Smiles.*) I was just being silly.

CLEO   I didn't hear what you said, though.

TED   It's ok.

CLEO   It's loud in here! (*Waits.*) Sorry, what'd you say? (*Beat.*) Go
   ahead . . .

TED   I know, but it's . . . now that I think it through it was pretty lame
   so I'm gonna spare you the embarrassment. Or, rather, me. Spare
   "me" the embarrassment. That's what I was saying. Or going to
   say . . .

CLEO   Oh, I see. Ok. (*Beat.*) Thanks for the tip.

TED   Don't mention it! (*Toasts her.*) Cheers! It's "Happy Hour!" Which
   goes from five to eight, which is *three* hours . . . so . . .

They drink. Stand for a moment. CLEO *glances over at him.*

CLEO   No, go on. Do it. I dare you!

TED   What's that?

CLEO   Embarrass yourself. Why not?

TED   Ummmmmm . . . a million reasons. Maybe more. I'm here with
   business clients—the guys over there, in the suits.

CLEO Who? The Asian guys? Those guys?

TED Yes. Japanese. Actually.

CLEO Is that not Asian anymore?

TED Ummmmm. Yeah, maybe so. Technically . . . but I think they prefer "Japanese." If one were to be ethnically sensitive . . .

CLEO Ok, fair enough . . . but they can't hear us, can they? Not way over here?

TED Ha! No, I don't think so . . .

CLEO Ok. Good. (*Waves to them.*) No offense, gentlemen!

TED *watches her do this and then sees that they seem to be responding back. He waves as well. Then bows. Again.* CLEO *watches this. Smiles. Bows to them as well.*

TED Anyway, yes, I gotta try to keep a clear head, but don't worry, I'm pretty good at it already, so . . . you know . . .

CLEO What's that?

TED Embarrassing myself! You should've seen me over at the Benihana's earlier—not the best with the ol' chopsticks!

She smiles at this. A little laugh. TED *laughs now, too.*

CLEO Really? You blew it, huh?

TED Oh, God yes! With all the— (*Miming how he ate.*) And I don't really need much help in that department, anyhow. Embarrassing myself. (*Beat.*) SO . . .

CLEO So then who's it gonna hurt? I don't know you . . . won't be able to pick you out of a line-up by tomorrow, with all the dirty martinis I'm drinking, so . . . go for it. (*Smiles.*) This is your big chance!

TED Yeah? Is that what this is?

CLEO . . . could be . . .

TED Ok, then. Just for fun.

CLEO Absolutely. I love fun. (*Beat.*) I am a good-time girl who loves me some fun! So: proceed.

TED I was gonna say when you stopped by me here, like you did a minute ago—to not fall in love with me. To be careful.

CLEO Really?

TED Yep. Just giving you fair warning!

CLEO I see. (*Beat.*) Well . . . thank you. Thanks.

TED My pleasure! 'Least I could do.

CLEO I mean, how was I to know, by stopping right here, that I might . . . actually . . .

TED Exactly!

CLEO That's very kind of you, sir!

TED I'm just that sort of guy! (*Smiles.*) I've got this sixth sense about things and it was just kind of rolling off of you . . . in waves . . . how much you were wanting me.

CLEO God, and I thought I had you fooled!

TED Sorry.

CLEO No, no . . . my mistake. Obviously. There's just no excuse for it. Forgive me.

TED Hey, it happens! Just the other day I was saying that to some-body . . . or someone—is one of those more right than the other? In proper grammar?—I'm never sure . . .

CLEO I dunno. (*Beat.*) Does it really, though? Happen to you a lot? People wanting you? Hitting on you? (*Beat.*) Yeah, prob'ly all the time . . . nice-looking guy like you.

TED Ha! (*Beat.*) Truthfully? No, almost never.

CLEO "Almost?"

TED Well, I met my girlfriend that way, but—sorry, no, wait, my fiancée, I'm supposed to call her my fiancée . . .

CLEO . . . okay . . .

TED And, actually, she wasn't really hitting on me but she did talk to me first, asked me the time and so, yeah . . . she made the first move, I would say . . . in a court of law.

CLEO Got it.

TED But other than her, though, no . . . not any other times in my life. Not even once . . . (*Beat.*) I've been "hit on" none times.

CLEO Ha! Except today.

TED Right! But . . . no, but you weren't really trying to . . . and I was kidding with you earlier. I was just playing around.

CLEO Oh. You were?

TED Yeah, I mean . . . yes! I was just . . . sorry, did I offend you or something? I didn't mean to. Honestly. I didn't.

CLEO No, no, not at all.

TED Good! Because that'd be . . . good. I'm glad.

CLEO About what? Not offending me . . . or . . .?

TED I guess! I'm a little bit drunk, so I'm not completely sure of anything that I'm saying at any one time but yeah . . . yes, I think so. I did not mean to make you mad. Or upset. Or . . . any of the above . . .

CLEO I'm not. At all.

TED Cool! You're very nice! (*Beat.*) And I mean that in a completely impartial and casual and mostly . . . non-sexual . . . sort of way.

CLEO Thanks. You too.

TED And you? You here with anybody, or . . .?

CLEO Nope. I'm alone. (*Beat.*) For now.

They smile and listen to the music. Bouncing to the beat.

TED Did you wanna go dance . . . or something?

CLEO Yeah?

TED Sure.

CLEO . . . ummmmmmmm . . .

TED I mean . . . go ahead . . . I can totally watch your drink for you. If you want.

CLEO Oh. (*Beat.*) But not with you?

TED What?

CLEO You're not asking me to . . . do you wanna go dance?

TED Wait . . . what? (*Beat.*) With *you*? (*Beat.*) Go out there and dance with you . . .?

CLEO General idea.

TED Ahhhhhhhhh . . .

CLEO It wouldn't suck. I promise.

TED No, I'm sure . . . of course . . . but . . .

CLEO It's cool. No worries. I get it. (*Smiles.*) Your lady . . . .

TED Yeah . . . probably not ideal.

CLEO It's just a dance.

TED Still. (*Pointing.*) People.

CLEO Okay. (*Beat.*) Got it.

TED Damn. (*Snaps his fingers.*) Sorry.

CLEO Too bad. (*She shimmies a little.*) I like this "house music" stuff . . .

TED That's what this is called? House Music?

CLEO Yep. Nice.

TED What's that mean exactly? That term?

CLEO What, "house music?"

TED I'm just curious. Isn't it a genre of . . .?

CLEO It's . . . like . . . you know . . . electric . . . or, I mean . . . not "electric," but "electronic." But also . . . (*Laughs.*) Shit! I don't know!

She pulls her phone out of her purse. Motions for TED.

CLEO Let's look it up. (*Searching the Internet.*) Hmmmmm . . .

TED I prefer "Google," but . . .

CLEO Yeah? I still use "Yahoo" for most everything. I'm kinda old school with all this techno stuff.

TED "Yahoo." Cool. That works. Occasionally. You could just . . . no. Nothing.

CLEO What?

TED It's not a big deal, but you're . . . if you do it that way—opening a new page each time, extra applications—it only slows things down. Easier if you . . . just . . .

CLEO You do it.

TED Oh. Sure. Yeah. (*Takes her phone.*) You would . . . just . . . if you move your finger over to—see? Like that.

CLEO Ahhh! Sweet! Nice shortcut, big guy . . .

TED Thank you. No biggie, but it just saves you a step or two . . . which adds up . . .

CLEO True. (*Beat.*) Is this your profession?

TED Ha! No . . . I'm in sales. I sell. Things. In the overseas market. Overseas stuff. Yep.

CLEO Oh, right, that's why you're . . . with that bunch. Over there. The Seven Samurai . . .

TED Ha! I'm "Ted," by the way. Or you can continue to use *big guy* if you prefer, but . . . yeah. Ted. My name.

CLEO "Cleo."

TED Oh. Nice. "Cle-o." (*Beat.*) Short for . . .?

CLEO Just that. "Cleo."

TED Interesting. Pretty. Not "Cleopatra?"

CLEO Nope! For a French girl. In a movie.

TED Oh . . . good.

CLEO Dying of cancer.

TED Oh . . . bad.

CLEO I mean, maybe. She's not sure. She thinks so . . . like, that's
the whole film . . . her as she waits to find out, for two hours, and
her going around Paris with friends . . . but hey . . . it's French, so
. . . it's really more about them smoking cigarettes and fucking
and, you know . . . that sort of deal. (*Beat.*) So, yeah. My mom
saw it in college, loved it, then I'm born and so BANG! That's me.

TED Right. (*Beat.*) Foreign film, I imagine.

CLEO Yes. Unless you're French, of course.

TED Right! Got it! "Cleo." (*Shakes her hand.*) Hey, Cleo, I'm Ted.
Hell-o. Anyway! (*Back to her phone.*) And there it is . . .
"Wikipedia." Now you can do whatever . . .

CLEO Got it! (*Reading.*) And . . . "House Music."

TED Great . . . let's see what they say.

CLEO Alright. Here goes. So . . . (*Reading.*) House Music . . . is a
genre of electronic dance music that . . . originated . . .

TED That's what you said. "Electronic."

CLEO Sorry?

TED No, I'll shut up. Sorry. Go for it.

CLEO . . . electronic dance music that originated in Chicago in
the early 1980s. Huh. It was initially popularized circa 1984 in
Chicago but fanned out to other major cities in North and South
America, as well as . . . (*Reads in silence.*) . . . early house
music was generally dance-based music . . . blah blah blah
. . . rhythms mainly provided by drum machines, off-beat hi-hat
cymbals and synthesized bass lines. Okay. Cool . . . (*Beat.*)
While House Music displayed several characteristics similar
to disco music . . . it was more electronic and minimalistic.
Agreed. It is kinda like disco, don't you think? A little? I mean
. . . similar . . .

TED Kind of. Yeah.

CLEO I think so, too. (*Reading.*) . . . House Music has also fused with several other genres creating various sub-genres . . .

TED Nice! "Sub-genres!"

CLEO Yes. "Sub-genres." (*Reading.*) . . . such as Euro House, Tech House, Electro House and—of course—Jump House.

TED Ahhhhh! I love "Jump House!"

CLEO Me, too!

TED Really?

CLEO No, I have no idea what the hell that is.

TED Me, either!

CLEO Good! I like you even more now! Because of that! (*Puts her phone away.*) Well . . . that answers that!

They nod at this new bit of info. He gets their drinks.

TED Daft Punk.

CLEO What? (*Listening.*) This is?

TED No, this isn't . . . I'm saying that band. The two helmet guys? Daft Punk? They're kind of this type music. "House Music."

CLEO Yes! Got it! (*Thinking.*) That's true . . .

She starts to sing a little bit of "Get Lucky" and, with some prompting, he joins her. They toast each other as they drink.

CLEO Alright, it's settled! No karaoke for us!

TED Ok! Excellent! (*Smiling.*) I'm gonna go get another drink . . .

CLEO What?

TED I'm dry. Out. I'm going to go get another one . . . the bar . . .

CLEO Oh . . . okay!

TED Want anything?

CLEO I would not hate you if you brought me one more little-tiny-baby dirty martini.

TED Ha! Can do!

She bows to him. TED *laughs and does the same. Heads off toward the bar.*

CLEO *looks in her bag. Pulls out her phone. Checks on her "look."* *Takes a selfie just as* TED *returns.*

CLEO . . . hey there.

TED Hi. (*Beat.*) What's up?

CLEO Nothing. Just swaying to this sub-genre of House Music, that's all.

TED Ha! Yeah . . . sounds like "Techno House" to me . . .

CLEO Could be, could be . . . I was thinking "Euro House," but you know—you might be right. (*Takes martini.*) Thank you, sir!

TED Pleasure!

CLEO Ummmmmmm! Now that is dirty! Yummy!

TED This is going really well! I'm so sorry that I'm not trying to pick you up!

CLEO Oh. So . . . you really aren't trying?

TED Nope, uh-uh. Not at all.

CLEO Ok.

TED Forgive me! It's got nothing to do with you. (*Beat.*) Did I mention I'm engaged?

CLEO You did, yes.

TED Good, because you're supposed to . . . if you are. Usually girls want you to mention it right off the top, first thing, so there: I am. Now you know. (*Beat.*) Some guys are not as forthcoming as me . . . but that seems wrong to me! Bad manners!

CLEO I agree!

TED Whereas I am getting it out in the open right up front . . . (*Shouts.*) "Hey, people! All of you can stop coming on to me right now! I am engaged here, so knock it off!"

CLEO Yeah! Back it up, bitches!! Back-it-up!! Thank you for that! (*Looks around.*) Everybody seems really relieved . . .

TED Well, I was getting a little fed up with all their crap! (*Turns to her.*) Especially you . . . you need to keep your hands off me, young lady!

CLEO Sorry! (*Hands held high.*) My bad . . .

TED I have little or no interest in you. "Little to none," is the actual phrase, I believe . . . little-to-no-or-none interest in you. (*Beat.*) Ok, I'm done . . . now . . . I think.

CLEO I see. (*Beat.*) Well, thank you . . . I guess?

TED Sure! Just being clear-ish about things.

CLEO Ok. But you're still standing here, so . . . you are kinda interested, though, right?

TED No, that's not . . . no! Absolutely not. I'm just trying to explain myself. That's all I was . . . right? Wait . . . lemme think. (*Beat.*) I'm . . . sure that I'm not . . . you're a really pretty—as in "attractive"— person but . . . no, I'm sure! I'm not interested in you!!

CLEO And thus your warning earlier. Right?

TED Exactly! Several warnings, in fact.

CLEO True. And . . . that was just . . . for . . .?

TED Your own good! Yes! To save you any sort of, like, heartbreak down the road . . . or later tonight, even. (*Beat.*) After.

CLEO Ahhhh. "After." (*Smiles.*) My favorite.

TED Yeah, you know . . . that's when people get a little bit weepy or whatever. "After."

CLEO You mean "after" all the . . . (*Makes a few hand gestures.*) . . . good stuff.

TED Yeah. Later tonight or even, maybe . . . the next morning if they decide to, you know.

CLEO That's when "people" get upset usually? Is that what you've discovered . . .?

TED It's been known to happen. I mean, to others. People who do those things . . . you know, behind the back of loved ones. Whom they've already made commitments to.

CLEO I see. But not you?

TED Virtually unheard of with me! And since I've been engaged . . . *not once.* (*Beat.*) That's zero number of times.

CLEO Interesting.

TED Simple fact, really. That's all. I'm the faithful type. (*Beat.*) Yep.

CLEO Which is why you warned me before?

TED Yes! Exactly! Now you're catching on!

CLEO It was more of a humanitarian gesture . . .

TED That type of thing! Not on like the scale of the U.N. or anything, but basically of a similar nature. It all springs from the desire to bring joy and do good things . . . same as them. Seriously. (*Beat.*) This is like one of those peacekeeping missions.

CLEO Ha! (*Beat.*) Ok, that's maybe a bit much! Let's be honest: this has been fun but if I said "Let's go upstairs right now" you would follow me like a lost little dog.

TED Nooooo! That is absolutely . . . not . . . true! (*Beat.*) No, you just . . . you kinda make me nervous. That's all. Little bit nervous.

CLEO Oh, really?

TED Yes! But I would not go upstairs.

CLEO And why's that?

TED Firstly, there's a drug store on the next level—street level—so that doesn't even make sense, unless that's a veiled signal for me to buy lube . . . which is . . . just . . .

CLEO Ha! NO!! (*Beat.*) You know what I mean! To my "house," then! With me. To my place.

TED Well . . . that's obviously . . . different.

CLEO And . . .?

TED What?

CLEO If I said that . . . "Let's get out of here and go to my place," you'd come with me, right? (*Beat.*) Wouldn't you? (*Beat.*) Ted?

TED I'd . . . no. I wouldn't! Plus, I'm here with people . . . my clients, which I already told you about. They're . . . Japanese . . .

CLEO Bullshit! And what does that have to do with anything? Them being Japanese? Or "Asians," technically?

TED . . . they wouldn't understand . . . they come from a very ancient culture. (*Beat.*) These people stab themselves all the time over practically nothing, so . . . no. I wouldn't.

CLEO I do not believe you.

TED Well, try me then. (*Beat.*) Go ahead!

CLEO Yeah, but . . . if I ask you now . . . you'll just reverse it and say "Yes'" and then I'll be stuck with you.

TED Oh, hey, thanks!

CLEO You know what I mean!

TED Ummmmmmmm, no, not really!

CLEO I was just making a point . . . before . . . not that I'd be "stuck" with you, but . . . what-ever! (*Laughing.*) You know what I mean!!

TED So wait, lemme get this—you don't really want to sleep with me or . . . do all the . . .?

CLEO . . . what?

TED The other stuff! What you did with your hand gestures . . . before . . . (*He tries to copy her earlier gestures.*) All of the . . . you know! The "good stuff."

CLEO Ahhhh. That stuff.

TED Hey, that's what you called it! I'm not trying to be all . . . sexy guy . . . here. You said it first!

CLEO That's true. I did.

TED You totally did. So . . .

CLEO But you would, though . . . right? If I asked you to. (*Beat.*) Come on, be honest!

TED Go upstairs? Go directly upstairs?

CLEO No, not to the drug store! (*Beat.*) If I asked you nicely to come home with me—

TED . . . and you made those hand gestures . . .

CLEO Yes! (*Smiles.*) If I did that . . . (*Makes a few more gestures.*) . . . then you would come. If I asked you to. Correct?

TED And you can promise that my fiancée would never find out . . .

CLEO . . . not ever . . .

TED And you will raise the child that will no doubt spring from our . . . unholy union . . . on your own without any help from me, be it financial or, or fiscal . . . or otherwise . . .

CLEO . . . those are essentially the same thing but alright . . . yes . . .

TED . . . then there's your answer! Right there.

CLEO What?

TED NO!! I can't!! (*Beat.*) See? You've already fallen in love with me! Why?! Why does it keep on happening to me?!! WHY?!!!

CLEO No, wait . . . I'm being serious now! (*Beat.*) I know, I know, your fiancée and all that other . . . guys always say that kinda thing, the due diligence bit, but I'm gonna just cut to the chase now. Okay? You're cute, I'm cute, so why don't we do this? Plus all those first bits you said—the stuff that really does worry you about babies or her finding out—I'm down with that. This would just be you and me. One night only. No last names. Just two strangers. (*Beat.*) This is not a rebate, there is no coupon attached here, so it's sort of a "now or never" thing. Ok? (*Beat.*) I know you're thinking, what-the-fuck or serial killer but hey . . . I'm lonely, I drank a lot . . . so I'm asking.

TED Get outta here! This is so shitty to do to somebody! (*Beat.*) Who are you? Do you know these guys . . . these Tokyo guys? I'm being serious now! What?! (*Beat.*) Wait . . . did Mike do this? Set you up to do this to me? From my office? (*Beat.*) Seriously! This had to be Mike . . . or Curtis, maybe. One of those two guys! Which one is it?!

CLEO Nope.

TED Seriously.

CLEO I don't know "Mike." Or "Curtis."

TED But this is . . . what's going on here?! This would never just . . . this doesn't happen!! Not to a guy like me. It doesn't. It's, like, some TV show thing, or . . . Ashton Kutcher jumps out now and surprises me. Right?! (*Beat.*) I'm being Punk'd!! DAFT-punked!!

CLEO . . . but you're still talking to me.

TED Yeah, but . . . I mean . . . Cleo. Come on!

CLEO Like I said, "now or never." And "never" is approaching like a . . . speeding train.

TED Cleo.

CLEO Ted. (*Beat.*) Up to you, buddy . . .

TED Then . . . you should . . . God!! Then you better go ahead and get on it, I suppose . . . yeah, I guess so.

CLEO . . . wait . . . I don't understand . . .

TED The train! That's coming. You should jump on board and take off . . . without me.

CLEO . . . ok. (*Beat.*) Wow. (*Exiting.*) Enjoy your night.

TED You too! (*To himself.*) "You too!" Are you a complete . . . assbag?! I mean . . . come on! "You too!" IDIOT!!

TED *stands by himself. Looking off into the crowd. Sipping his drink. After a long moment* CLEO *returns. Standing right next to him.*

CLEO Don't say anything, just listen. This is your choice and I respect it. I do. All I want to say is that I'm . . . you know . . . I am surprised. That's all. You caught me off-guard, and I'm not saying this because I think I'm so amazing or anything—I mean, I am kind of great but that's beside the point—I'm just . . . I want you to know that I think you are . . . I dunno . . . I think that was cool of you and rare, you turning me down like that, and I just wanted to say that she's a very lucky girl and . . . yeah. That's all. Very very lucky.

TED Thank you. That's really nice of you to say.

CLEO You're welcome.

TED Honestly. It is.

CLEO I just thought you should know . . . (*Beat.*) Okay, seriously. Last chance! And "what happens in Cleo, stays in Cleo." (*Waits.*) Wow! Shit, that's my best line ever. Ok, I'll give you ten seconds and then I'm outta here! Promise . . . So? (*Beat.*) Okay, I'll count it out. Fine. One. Two. Three. (*Beat.*) Four. Five. Six. (*To* TED.) Seriously? (*Beat.*) Seven. Eight. (*To* TED.) Come on! Jesus! (*Beat.*) Nine . . . (*To* TED.) I mean . . . this is just . . . (*Beat.*) Fine. (*Beat.*) Ten. That's ten. "The end." God, you're tough!! (*Beat.*) Alright then. I'm going now. I'll . . . just . . . yeah. (*Beat.*) . . . and . . . you're not even gonna ask me for my number or the . . . like, my facebook . . . or nothing. Twitter? (*Beat.*) Nope. Nothing.

TED I'm . . . I want to . . . I mean, sorta . . . but no. I'm not going to because that would be . . . you know. I can't. (*Smiles.*) I mean, if my girlfriend was out and some guy was all up in her "grill" or whatever . . . you know? (*Beat.*) Not that I'm feeling that about you . . . that you're up in my grill or, or, my, you know, my . . . face . . .

I don't . . . I really don't! (*Beat.*) But . . . you know what I mean. It wouldn't be right.

CLEO No, that's true. It wouldn't be. At all. OK. (*Beat.*) BUT . . . what if . . . this was a set-up, that I've known your girlfriend for years, that she's my . . . good . . .

TED . . . my fiancée, you mean . . .

CLEO Right, yeah, your fiancée—listen to me—if I told you that we went to college together . . . her and me . . .

TED . . . no . . .

CLEO Yes . . . and just the other day we ran into each other downtown and over lunch she asked me to check up on you, to approach you when you're at work or on a business dinner, after you'd had a few drinks, and see if you would go to bed with me—just to be sure that she can trust you before marrying you, she had me do that . . . what would you do if that was the truth? Hmm?

TED Oh.

CLEO Or if this was, like, reincarnation, or I'm the ONE person you were waiting for all of your life . . .? What would you do if that's what is actually happening here . . . instead of us just accidentally bumping into each other by chance on this lonely Thursday evening? Hmmmm? (*Beat.*) What then? (*Beat.*) Ted?

TED . . . I would . . . you know . . . I'd have to give that some pretty . . . serious . . . thought.

CLEO I know *I* would. I mean, if it were me. *I'd* give it some pretty deep and serious thought . . . and I'd do it this very second. Right-the-fuck now . . . before this . . . beautiful, mysterious, wonderful creature standing here in front of you—who just might turn out to be the absolute LOVE of your life—is gone. That's what I'D do . . . if I were you.

TED That's some . . . good . . . solid . . . advice there.

CLEO And to be fair—regardless of the rest of this, you and your
fiancée and all that other shit I just threw out right now—you
haven't even seen me do this yet . . .

TED What?

She puts a finger in his mouth then in her own. Sucks it.

CLEO That.

TED Ahh. "That." (*Beat.*) No . . . I didn't yet have that important . . .
bit of . . . info . . .

CLEO No, you didn't. Did you?

TED No.

CLEO Too bad. (*Beat.*) Or this. (*Gets closer.*) Bet you didn't know
this, either . . .

Kisses him until he stops and breaks free of her. Steps away.

TED No. (*Beat.*) I didn't. So obviously I'd need to . . . you know . . .
factor all that in there, too.

CLEO "Obviously." (CLEO *steps to him*—TED *backs up.*) . . . have fun
with your clients.

CLEO *touches his mouth and smiles. Exits.* TED *watches her go then
stands alone in silence. Finally he says:*

TED That's . . . are you kidding me? I mean . . . are you fucking
kidding me?!!! SHIT!!!! What was that?! What the hell was that?!
(*Suddenly,* TED *pulls out his phone.*) . . . come on, come on . . .!
(*Waits.*) Hey, hi there, honey! Hello!! I was just . . . yeah, I know
it's still loud . . . I know . . . what? Ummmm, no, they're still
partying away! No, I still don't know the name of the song . . .
I wanted to call you because . . . well, I really miss you . . . I do.
(*Beat.*) No, I wish I was there, too. No. Believe me, I really do.
But listen. (*Beat.*) Hmmm? What? You're already on the phone?

With who? Oh! Well, say "Hi" to your mom for me . . . can you call me back? WHY? Because I miss you . . . and I love you . . . and I need you . . . oh. Ok. Sure. 'Bye . . . 'bye. (*Beat.*) 'Bye.

He stands there. Alone. Music blaring. Looking around the bar and not knowing what to do. Waves at the other guys again. Signals to them. Bows. Tries to dial again. Bows.

He slowly turns and looks off toward where CLEO *has gone. Lowers his phone while he stares off into the distance.*

Silence. Darkness.

I'M GOING TO STOP PRETENDING (THAT I DIDN'T BREAK YOUR HEART)

I'M GOING TO STOP PRETENDING (THAT I DIDN'T BREAK YOUR HEART) had its world premiere as part of the AdA "Desire" project at the Venice Biennale in Venice, Italy, in August 2014.
It was directed by Nathalie Fillion.

HER   Emilia Verginelli
SHE   Elisa Alessandro

Silence. Darkness.

Two women are somewhere. At home, probably. A house or an apartment. A place where they both live. For now.

One sits while the other busies herself with setting a table for dinner. Plates, glasses, silverware. The works.

After a moment:

SHE . . . so . . . then . . .

HER . . .

SHE . . . what . . .?

Silence as one of the women thinks about what to say for a long moment. Finally:

HER I'm sorry.

SHE Uh-huh.

HER I am, though.

SHE Okay.

HER I *am* sorry. I don't really know what else to say . . . other than that, but . . . "sorry."

SHE You're sorry?

HER Yes.

SHE Alright.

HER *Very* sorry, actually . . .

SHE Why?

HER Just . . . you know . . .

SHE No. *Why?*

HER   Because of . . . whatever! How things are. How they're going.

SHE   You mean . . .?

HER   Between us. How things are between us now. Or have ended up. *Here.* Like this . . .

Silence again as one woman thinks about this. Weighs it out in her head. After a moment:

SHE   Doesn't have to be that way, though.

HER   What?

SHE   Just . . . I mean . . . so you know: it does not have to end like this. The way it's going right now. (*Beat.*) Not from *my* side . . . not at all. (*Beat.*) It doesn't.

HER   . . .

SHE   *What?*

HER   Nothing. No. (*Beat.*) I mean, that's *easy* to say, but . . . you know . . . it's not true. (*Beat.*) It's not.

SHE   Isn't it?

HER   No.

SHE   Why?

HER   Because . . . it's . . . just . . . *because.*

SHE   Yeah. "Because." That's all you've said to me so far about it. "Be-cause."

HER   You *know* why.

SHE   No . . .

HER   . . . *yes* . . .

SHE   No, I don't. I really don't.

HER   Fuck.

SHE   *What?*

HER   I just . . .

SHE   No, what're you . . .?

HER   You *know*.

SHE   Not really, I mean . . .

HER   Oh, come on . . .

SHE   What? I don't . . . I think that we're . . .

HER   I-DON'T-LOVE-YOU-ANY-MORE! (*Beat.*) *There*. (*Beat.*) Is it
better if I say it that way? To your face? (*Beat.*) Is it?

*They both stop for a moment. Waiting to see how the other person
responds. Finally:*

SHE   . . . I guess.

HER   Yeah? That was better? (*Beat.*) Raising my voice and getting . . .
all . . .?

SHE   I guess so. (*Beat.*) *Yes.*

HER   *Why*? Why do people need to hear things like that . . . in person
and *so* . . . to make something feel real? (*Beat.*) Seriously?

SHE   I don't know.

HER   Neither do I! I've never understood that, why it's so important
to . . . you know . . . to do that. To *shout*. Why people want that.

SHE   I dunno, but they do. They just do and so it's . . . (*Beat.*) You
know they do.

HER   Yeah.

SHE   Right?

HER   Yes. (*Beat.*) We're masochists, I guess.

SHE   No, it's just . . . whatever. Human nature or something. (*Beat.*)
To want *contact*.

HER   Fine.

SHE   I'm not making it up. People do need it.

HER   OKAY. (*Beat.*) Anyway, I already said it. (*Beat.*) Before. (*Beat.*)
Right? (*Beat.*) Not that you liked hearing it . . . but . . .

SHE   No, you did. You said it. (*Beat.*) Said it one time and then again.

Now. (*Beat.*) You *screamed* it at me and this time I heard you.

HER I mean . . . did you not believe me the first time or what? (*Beat.*) Hmmmmm?

SHE No, I did.

HER . . . I *wonder* . . .

SHE I *did*! I just . . . I figured maybe you'd say it one more time and hear yourself and then . . . I dunno. Really *think* about what you're doing here—doing to me and, you know, to "us"—and that you'd wake up or whatever. Wake up and see what this means to our relationship and . . . just . . . maybe . . . stop. (*Beat.*) That's all. (*Beat.*) I guess I hoped that you'd . . . stop. This.

HER "Stop" what?

SHE I-don't-know! Stop saying that or feeling it or something. Just "stop." That's all. (*Beat.*) Stop being that way.

HER How can I? (*Beat.*) Seriously, *how*? (*Beat.*) I mean, when it's true. When I actually do feel that way? About you?

SHE . . .

HER I don't love you anymore, Kim. I'm sorry. I *wish* that I did. I've *tried* to . . . pushed myself to feel something for you . . . but I don't. I don't love you and that's . . . I'm sorry, but it's true.

SHE You really don't?

HER No.

SHE Not even just a little? (*Beat.*) A little bit? (*Beat.*) A *teensy* little bit?

HER No. Sorry. (*Beat.*) I used to . . . back in the day or whatever . . . in school and stuff . . . but . . .

SHE . . . not any more.

HER No. (*Beat.*) I don't.

SHE Okay. No, I get it . . . (*Beat.*) *Got* it.

HER Sorry.

SHE Stop saying that! I *know* you're sorry . . . you've said it a *hun-dred* times so I'm aware that you're . . . whatever . . . "sorry." (*Beat.*) I look over at you at dinner or wherever . . . some restaurant . . . and you've always got that look on your face now . . . (*She makes a look.*) "Sorry." "I'm sorry." "I'm *so* so sorry."

HER I am, though.

SHE ALRIGHT, OKAY! YOU'RE "SORRY!" I-GET-IT!

Another silence falls over them as they wait for someone to speak again. After a beat:

HER Maybe we should do this later . . .

SHE No! No way . . . that's . . .

HER . . . but . . .

SHE Let's just . . . no. *Now.* We should get this over with now. *Right* now.

HER Fine.

SHE Here and now.

HER I said "fine." (*Beat.*) So? (*Beat.*) DO YOU *HAVE* TO DO THAT? HMM? (*Beat.*) DO YOU *HAVE* TO SET THE TABLE *RIGHT* NOW? I mean . . .

SHE Yeah, I do! *YES!* (*Beat.*) It helps me, ok? (*Beat.*) Doing this calms me so that's why I'm . . . don't worry about it. Alright?

Silence as one of them thinks about what to say next as the other continues to arrange table settings. Then:

HER So . . . are we gonna . . . ummmmmm . . . you know?

SHE What?

HER Nothing. I just . . . do you wanna continue living here, or should you . . . or *I*—do we keep doing this, living like this, or do we . . . what? (*Beat.*) What's next?

SHE I dunno. You tell me.

HER Ahhhhhh . . . well . . .

SHE You want me to go, right? (*Beat.*) I mean, in a perfect world . . . what would happen? I'd leave, right? (*Beat.*) *Right*? (*Beat.*) Tess?

HER I suppose.

SHE Of *course* I would.

HER Yeah. (*Beat.*) *Yes*. (*Beat.*) I suppose so. If things were . . . you know . . .

SHE Because this is your place . . .

HER Right, but . . . no . . . not just that . . .

SHE But it is. It's your house. Your *home*. You've always made that pretty clear . . . so that's the truth. Right? (*Beat.*) *Right*?

HER Right.

SHE Okay, good. Fine. So just *say* it then . . .

HER Yes. (*Beat.*) That'd be best. (*Beat.*) If you would go. (*Beat.*) At some point.

SHE "In a perfect world."

HER Uh-huh.

SHE But, I mean, to be fair—this is actually pretty far from perfect. (*Beat.*) Don't you think? Our situation here? (*Beat.*) *Tess*?

One of them looks at the other and pauses before saying:

HER I suppose so. Yes.

SHE Yeah. (*Beat.*) "Perfect" would've been us together forever. Like we talked about. That'd be "perfect." To *me*. That's what a "perfect world" would be. (*Beat.*) So . . .

HER . . . okay . . .

SHE "Perfect" is what you *promised* me before all this . . .

HER Well, no . . . that's . . . not . . .

SHE Ummmmm. Kinda. Yeah. (*Beat.*) How you said it'd be. For us. *Before* I did this . . .

HER   . . .

SHE   What I've done. To myself. For you.

HER   I *know*. (*Beat.*) We said a *lot* of stuff. We both did. (*Beat.*) Along the way . . .

SHE   Yep. We *sure* did. (*Beat.*) Along the way.

HER   . . . but . . .

SHE   Especially you. A lot of promises to me. A *lot*. (*Beat.*) Before.

HER   Okay, okay! (*Beat.*) *Okay.* (*Beat.*) I know.

SHE   Promises that don't seem to mean shit anymore, though . . . do they? (*Beat.*) Right?

HER   Ummmmmm . . . that's not very fair . . .

SHE   How? How is that not fair?

HER   . . . *because* . . .

SHE   Don't say *that*! Not "because." Alright? Not just "because" again . . . (*Beat.*) You have something more to say then say it, say it to *me*. To my face or whatever but not any more of this bullshit "because."

A little pause as one of them starts to say something but stops.
Rethinks her thought. Then:

HER   Fine. Alright. (*Beat.*) What do you want me to say, then? (*Beat.*) Hmmmmm? (*Beat.*) What?

SHE   Anything. Something. (*Beat.*) *Some*-thing.

Silence while one of them tries to regroup. To think of what to say now. After a bit:

HER   So, yes, we made . . . like . . . pledges to each other. Promises. Things like that . . .

SHE   Yes.

HER   And that's not . . . I'm not saying that did not happen . . . but . . . a lot of that talk was you being . . . *forcing* me to . . . you know . . .

SHE What?

HER Just . . . *nothing.* (*Beat.*) Forget it.

SHE No, *what*? Explain . . .

HER Things . . . just . . . happen! Change. People do and that's . . .
I dunno. That's life. It is. Life sometimes gets very . . . you know . . .
we grow, or, or . . . shit . . . yeah. "Grow." Grow *up* or *out* or—how
else can you use that word?—in some . . . other direction . . .
come *on,* you know that's true! We do. People move on and they
. . . it happens every day! Every *second* somewhere in the world
and I don't wanna have to feel so . . . guilty about this. I really
don't. I've grown up and not just that, "up," but also . . .

SHE "Away from."

HER Yes! We've *grown away* from each other . . . (*Beat.*) We have.
(*Beat.*) Couples do.

SHE Or closer.

HER Ok, yes. Sometimes . . . but . . .

SHE That can happen, too, you know . . . if they try. (*Beat.*) They can
get *closer*.

HER Or "apart."

SHE Or "together."

HER OKAY, OKAY . . . SHIT! *BAD* ANALOGY!! SORRY!!! It doesn't
matter . . .

SHE No, it's fine . . . it's fine . . .

HER No, obviously, it's not . . . whatever. (*She stops.*) You're gonna
make me *pay* for this, aren't you? Of *course* you are. I get it.
(*Beat.*) I'm the one who wants something . . . something else in life
and so for that I have to pay. *I*-pay-you. (*Beat.*) Right?

SHE What?

HER . . . just . . . stop . . .

SHE No, what do you mean? (*Beat.*) *What*?

HER Supposedly I deserve it.

SHE Do you?

HER I guess so. (*Beat.*) Yes. (*Beat.*) I fell out of love with you and so now I have to pay some sort of . . . like . . . "price" for that so I will. (*Beat.*) Tell me what it is and we can just be done with it. (*Beat.*) Go on . . . tell me. (*Beat.*) Go ahead, Kim.

Silence before she answers. She thinks about this very carefully and eventually says:

SHE I think you're right. I think there is a price for what you've done . . . or not done . . . or whatever you wanna call it. (*Beat.*) Yes, I do. (*Beat.*) People get away with too much . . . just walk away from all the messes we make and that's wrong. It *is*.

HER So tell me what it is, then. Tell me what I have to do now to balance this out . . .

SHE Nothing.

HER "Nothing?"

SHE I mean, just *this* . . . what you're doing . . . (*Beat.*) You've gotta live with it. From now on. (*Beat.*) *That's* the cost. *That* is the penalty for your . . . bad behavior . . .

HER Wait! God! *Really*? I mean . . . I know it's serious and all that, but . . . *really*? You are gonna call this "bad behavior" now?

SHE Well . . . what else is it? (*Beat.*) Honestly?

HER It's *life*! This is what happens to us!!

SHE Not everybody . . .

HER No, not everybody! NO! AGREED! But to a few us—a *lot* of us, actually—and lots of them just . . . you know . . . go on living. They do. They make a go of it and start over, on their own or with someone new and . . . that's . . . God! I dunno! That's how it works. When it doesn't work. It works out in some-other-way for

. . . those of us who're just *bumbling* around down here on the surface of the Earth. (*Beat.*) We fall in and out of love and try not to hold grudges or, or, or . . . rub people's noses in their own dirt . . . we try not to do it because it's bad karma and not nice and just . . . plain . . . uncool . . . to do that. Not cool. At all. (*Beat.*) I've been with you for *twelve* years . . . since *college* . . . and I, fuck, you know . . . I *told* you!! Didn't I?! *Warned* you that this could happen, that I might not be with you forever, or, or—you know that's true!! YOU KNOW THAT!!! (*Beat.*) "Love" shouldn't be a punishment, ok?! It's not some "death sentence" or, like, like . . . *irreversible*! It's just not.

SHE I know.

HER But you just . . . keep . . . going! You . . . you know what you do! You *do* that to me!!

SHE I *know.*

HER You've *always* been pushing . . . pushing me to be with you . . . be yours. To always be yours and to never, you know, pursue the other part of me. That *side* that's not . . .

SHE Yes.

HER I *DON'T* LOVE MEN! I *never* have! I dated a few—enough to know—and I just . . . that's not me. For *me*. (*Beat.*) I told you that . . . I told you that was the case and yet you stuck with me, saying things would be ok and that we could . . . that maybe we'd be able to . . . to . . . I don't know! (*Beat.*) Look, I'm just . . . tired, and, and . . . this is . . .

SHE *What*?

HER For *years* I told you that! We made good friends, years ago, when we first met . . . I liked that. Us as "friends." But that too, you pushed . . . you pushed us to be more than that . . . something else. Some other thing. Some . . . (*Gesturing.*) *This.*

SHE Ummmmm . . . you suggested it first. (*Beat.*) To be fair.

HER . . . *no* . . .

SHE Yes. (*Beat.*) You did, too. (*Beat.*) YES.

HER Which part?

SHE Not us as a *couple* maybe, but . . . sex. Trying it together. Us having sex.

HER Yeah, ok, but . . . I did that . . . because . . .

SHE Why? "Because" why?

HER To *see*! To just see if . . . maybe I was . . . who knows? "Wrong." "Mistaken." (*Beat.*) That was *me* trying. Trying to make a go of this with you. *For* you. Because *you* wanted it *so* bad. Wanted me so much . . . so I did that. For you. (*Beat.*) I tried it, okay? I did. (*Beat.*) I *tried*.

SHE And you hated it . . .

HER NO! Shit, why does it have to be so . . . black or white or . . . just . . . *no*! No, no, no! I did not hate it with you, I just didn't like it much. Care for it. Want it for the rest of my life. (*Beat.*) Sex with a *man*. (*Beat.*) It's not for me . . .

SHE Yeah, I know . . . you have made that very clear. Over the years. VERY CLEAR.

HER Okay, but I did *try*. (*Beat.*) I *did*.

SHE True. Closed your eyes and tried . . .

HER . . . no . . .

SHE Grit your teeth and tried . . .

HER . . . that's not . . .

SHE Held your breath and tried . . .

HER Stop! That's *not* true! (*Beat.*) I just . . .

SHE You love women. That's all. (*Beat.*) Right? (*Beat.*) Isn't that right?

HER I do.

SHE You love women and not men.

HER That's right.

SHE I should've believed you in the first place, but I just . . . I wanted you . . . *so* much. Since that first lecture we were in . . . I just . . . I wanted you to be mine. Wanted you to *want* me . . . to be *with* me . . . (*Beat.*) But I should've listened. That's what I should've done.

HER Maybe so.

SHE I should've heard what you kept saying over and over . . . and *over* . . .

HER . . . I did try to . . . you know . . .

SHE I *know*! (*Beat.*) I know that. (*Beat.*) And that's why *I* did *this*. Changed myself . . .

HER Yes.

SHE I became this. (*Indicates.*) I did this . . . for you. (*Indicates.*) *All* of it was for you.

HER I'M AWARE OF THAT! Okay? I *know*. I get it and I'm . . . very . . . *very* . . .

SHE "Sorry?"

HER Yes.

SHE You're "sorry."

HER I am.

SHE You feel bad. (*Beat.*) Right? (*Beat.*) "Bad."

HER I do. Yes. (*Beat.*) But it's also . . . you know . . . it's not just my fault . . . it's really not. (*Beat.*) People change.

SHE Some quite literally. Like me.

HER *Please*! I'm trying to talk to you now. Like grown-ups. Like grown-up people do.

SHE Okay. (*Smiling.*) And what is it they say to each other? When that happens? These grown-ups? (*Beat.*) "I'm sorry you went and chopped your dick off, but tough luck . . ."

HER No . . .

SHE "Better luck next time . . ."

HER . . . no . . .

SHE "As luck would have it . . ."

HER Stop.

SHE "At least you're kind of pretty . . ." Something like that?! Hmm-mmm?!

HER STOP IT! *STOP*! *IT*!

One of them bursts into tears. Sits there. Sobbing. After a little while they try to go on:

SHE I'm sorry . . . I just . . .

HER I know.

SHE I love you. That's all.

One of them is about to answer but stops herself. Then:

HER . . . I know you do.

SHE "I know you do." (*Laughs.*) Not even just a crumb, huh? Not even a quick little "love you, too" for me . . . just this once? (*Beat.*) No? Nothing?

HER . . . I can't . . .

SHE "Can't" what?

HER If I do that . . . say that to you . . . you will latch onto it . . . grab hold of it like some *life preserver* in the ocean . . .

SHE Oh *really . . .*?

HER Yes! You *know* you will. Come on! Like it's some . . . piece of *debris* out in the Atlantic . . . and hold me to it . . . remember the date and the time and the place and throw it right back in my face a dozen times over the next ten conversations! (*Beat.*) That's why I can't say that to you . . . not even once. (*Beat.*) I'm sorry, but . . . I know you. *How* you are. (*Beat.*) It's true . . .

SHE Wow.

HER I don't mean to be hurtful.

SHE *No*?

HER Not at all.

SHE . . . then you probably shouldn't say stuff like that any more. (*Beat*.) You know why? (*Beat*.) BECAUSE IT FUCKING HURTS! It hurts and it stings and you should think twice before you *ever* say it again!! Okay?!!!

HER Sorry.

SHE Yeah! I remember! You're *sorry* . . .

HER I am.

SHE Ok, ok. You're sorry. (*Beat*.) So . . . just for the record: what don't you like? (*Beat*.) Specifically . . .

HER What?

SHE About *me*! About all the work I've done on myself . . . my *body* . . . on changing me . . .

HER Oh God, please . . . don't . . .!

SHE No, just so I'll know! For the future . . .

HER That's not . . .

SHE Oh come *on*!! You *allowed* it to happen in the first place . . . so you can tell me now, I can take it! *Promise*!! (*Beat*.) Go ahead.

HER I don't wanna do this . . .

SHE Do it for me! I don't care what you want for once! THINK ABOUT *ME*!! OKAY?!! (*Beat*.) So, what is it, my face? Is it the way my face has turned out? *Is* it? (*Beat*.) Or the way I do my hair? (*Beat*.) Is that it?

HER . . . no . . .

SHE "No" you do or don't like it?

HER I like it.

SHE So, my make-up? (*Beat*.) I can change that. My make-up. Too much? I can change it . . .

HER It's not that.

SHE No?

HER No. You're very beautiful. (*Beat.*) Pretty at least. (*Beat.*) I like your face . . .

SHE Okay. Fine. (*Opens her blouse.*) My tits? (*Beat.*) Is that it? (*Beat.*) *Yes*? (*Beat.*) It is them or do you like them?

HER Yes. (*Beat.*) They're nice. Yes.

SHE Not huge. You never said you wanted me to make them huge . . .

HER That's not . . . no. I like them very much.

SHE They're natural.

HER I know.

SHE I mean . . . as natural as being all pumped full of shit to make it happen can be . . .

HER Right.

SHE But I could still change them. Add a bit more to them. If you wanted me to . . .

HER I don't. (*Beat.*) *Please.* (*Beat.*) I don't.

SHE Okay. (*Lifts up her skirt.*) And here? Do you like me down here? The way I feel? (*Grabs her hand and makes her feel her body.*) Just . . . there. Come on. *Touch* me.

HER . . . yes . . .

SHE You do?

HER I mean . . . it feels normal . . .

SHE Does it?

HER Yes. (*Beat.*) The way it should.

SHE Like other woman you've had?

HER Yes.

SHE It *does*?

HER Yes, it does.

SHE Like your own, even? Is this as nice as your own? (*Beat.*)

Because I think yours is *beautiful*. I *love* it. I've always loved it and so . . . you know . . . I just wonder . . .

HER Kim . . . *PLEASE* . . .

SHE Just-tell-me!

HER Yes. They did a good job.

SHE It feels okay?

HER I think so. Yes.

SHE And it looks . . . it's not strange-looking or anything? Right? (*Beat.*) *Right*?

HER No.

SHE I could shave it or do . . . whatever . . . if it makes you happier. (*Beat.*) I would do anything to make you happier. You know that, right? Any. Thing. (*Beat.*) I *would*. (*Beat.*) With hair grown in I think it looks good but I can . . . you know . . . whatever you want I can do. I *can*. (*Beat.*) For you.

HER That's not . . . no, it's fine . . .

SHE But I would. I'd do that.

HER I know you would.

SHE Right. Fine. (*Beat.*) And my ass? (*Flicks up her skirt to show her ass.*) And legs? All that shit? (*Beat.*) No problems?

HER No. (*Beat.*) *Honestly*. (*Beat.*) You have a very nice body . . .

SHE Thanks. (*Beat.*) Thank you, Tess.

HER You do, though. Really.

SHE But: (*Beat.*) Right? (*Beat.*) *BUT*:

HER What?

SHE *What* is it? What is it about me that you don't like? Or want? Or whatever it is . . .

HER It's . . . just . . . (*Beat.*) You're just . . .

SHE *What*?! (*Beat.*) Is there someone else?

HER No.

SHE You can tell me . . .

HER There isn't.

SHE Do you promise? (*Beat.*) YOU PROMISE?!

HER KIM, STOP IT! *STOP*!! (*Beat.*) I *promise*.

SHE . . . God! It's like you don't get it or something . . . like . . . you're . . . I DUNNO!!

HER What?

SHE *This*! This is *it* for me! You are! *Us*!!

HER Look, I know that we're . . . not . . .

SHE No, there's no explaining this away . . . this, right here—ME— this "new" me is it! This is who I am now . . . this is who I *have* to be. Who I *want* to be as well, but, yeah . . . this is it. I am here now and this is . . . I *can't* go back! I mean, I literally *cannot* go back . . . you know that! Right?! (*Beat.*) RIGHT?!!

HER . . . ok, but . . .

SHE No BUTS! There are no BUTS here!! I am this person now— who you see in front of you and there is *no* going back . . . (*Beat.*) . . . whether you like it or not, whether you are attracted to me or, or . . . you *desire* me or *despise* me . . . I am all I have now! All I have to offer you!!! (*Indicating.*) *This* right *here*!!!

HER I *know* that! I *know* . . . (*Beat.*) Just . . . please, don't be . . . so . . . (*Beat.*) *God*!!

SHE What?

HER Don't say it like it's . . . *so* . . .

SHE *What*?!

HER I DON'T KNOW! *SOMETHING*!! Like I *owe* you something because of this . . . like I'm to *blame* or . . . like . . . in *debt* to you because of a choice *you* made . . . a choice that . . .

SHE We made! WE DID THIS TOGETHER! *WE*!! We talked about this and, and we read the literature . . . spoke to the doctors and—

watched those videos—dozens and dozens of videos about all this—*we* did that. As a *couple*. (*Beat.*) I'm not making this up or trying to make you feel bad but I did this for us, not on my own . . . all the *pain* . . . those operations that I . . . you were there! You *saw* what I did but I was willing to do that. For *US*.

HER   Ok, ok, OK!! Fine, but . . . you just keep on and on like there's only one answer here . . . like we *have* to do just this *one* thing and I don't believe that, I don't! Sorry, but . . . (*Beat.*) There isn't just one possibility here . . . we can discuss it and . . . I'm just saying that it isn't final . . .

SHE   IT *IS* FINAL! IT IS!! *THIS* IS IT!!!

HER   No, that isn't true . . . it isn't!! I know you took a major step with this . . . it was a very *major* . . . I *know* . . . but that doesn't mean that . . . I'm somehow . . . *responsible* . . . (*Beat.*) Okay?! That's all I'm saying . . . is that . . . I don't even know *what* I'm saying any more! (*Beat.*) I dunno. I'm exhausted.

SHE   So . . . what is it, then? Hmmm? (*Beat.*) Tess? If it's not my body or my face . . . if I'm now a woman and not a man and that's what you *like,* what you *want* most in your life in terms of a relationship . . . then what is it? (*Beat.*) What am I doing wrong? Hmmmm?! (*Beat.*) Tell me. Come on. (*Beat.*) Come *on*! Tell me *that* much! (*Beat.*) Say it . . .

HER   It's . . . just . . . you. (*Beat.*) I don't want you any more. (*Beat.*) Ok? (*Beat.*) *There*. (*Beat.*) I just don't want *you* . . .

This stops one of them cold. They wait for a second to let this moment of tension pass. Then:

SHE   Oh. (*Beat.*) You . . . just . . .

HER   . . . I'm sorry . . .

SHE   *Oh.*

HER And I can't . . . fix that! I thought that I could . . . that time might
. . . or what you've done would help . . . but . . . no. (*Beat.*) Sorry.

SHE So . . . you like girls . . . but just not "this" girl? (*Beat.*) Right?
(*Beat.*) Is that right? (*Beat.*) Not this "girl" that I've tried so hard to
become for you? Yes? (*Beat.*) Yes? (*Beat.*) *YES*?

HER I guess so. (*Beat.*) I'm . . . (*Beat.*) Yes.

*They sit for another minute in silence. Staring at each other. A nod
from her as she understands now. Finally.*

SHE *. . . ok . . .*

One of them gets up and moves away. Toward another room.

SHE . . . I made us a salad for tonight. Is that alright? Didn't feel like
cooking.

HER Sure.

SHE It's hot, so . . . I thought that'd be good.

HER Yes.

SHE . . . alright then.

HER Alright.

SHE Fine.

HER Fine.

SHE Fine. (*Beat.*) . . . let's eat.

*She starts to go. Brushes past the other woman who puts out a hand
to touch her but just misses her. She leaves and one of them is left
alone in the room.*

Silence. Darkness.

EXHIBIT 'A'

EXHIBIT 'A' had its world premiere as part of "Walking the Tightrope" (a collection of anti-censorship plays) at Theatre Delicatessen in London, England, in January 2015.
It was directed by Cressida Brown.

ARTIST   Syrus Lowe
SUBJECT   Kelly Burke

Silence. Darkness.

Lights up to reveal the SUBJECT. *Down on all fours (or bent over a table or whatever works). Tape over his mouth. Tied up. Looking out at us.*

After a moment the ARTIST *walks out and stands over him (or next to him or whatever works).*

ARTIST   . . . good evening and welcome. Thank you for coming. I'm glad you all could make it here. Much appreciated. With so many entertainment choices available to you in a city of this size, it's nice to see it when people make the choice to actively support the arts. I love that. I really do. I dig it. Makes me feel good . . . good about what I do and why I do it. (*Beat.*) I'm an artist and so this . . . (*Indicating the audience.*) . . . seeing all of you here, being a part of this . . . it means a lot. (*Beat.*) Believe me, seeing those others out front with their signs and placards, screaming shit at me when I arrived . . . I understand, I do. The arts bring out the passion in us and that's good. That is great. But come on, it's also scary! I mean, those people are . . . they want me to stop. Or worse. To die. To be dead. DEAD. For what? For being an *artist*? For making "*art*?" And I know, I know, I am touching on a subject here that is volatile—taboo, even—but *that's* the point! This needs to be exposed . . . examined . . . evaluated. (*Beat.*) And where better than here? In a sacred space like this one: an art gallery. Just because it's scary and tough, it shouldn't stop us from interacting . . . from us coming together in a moment such as this one—as artist, subject and audience—and exploring it. Should it?

The ARTIST *starts to unbuckle his belt and remove it. Keeps one eye on the audience.*

ARTIST Maybe you've heard about me . . . what I've been working on this year. On this. Right here. (*Pointing to the* SUBJECT.) I've been working on this for the past several years, actually. I mean, not just this one—this subject over here . . . but this exhibit. My "Exhibit 'A'." That's what I call it. "Exhibit '*A*'." (*He smiles.*) I was gonna call it ASS or MANHOOD or something like that but . . . you know . . . it seemed a little bit obvious.

The ARTIST *pulls off his shirt now, revealing his bare chest to the audience.*

ARTIST To be honest . . . I don't think there's anything we can't do in an art gallery—once you call it "art," give something that label— then it should be safe and off limits. Whatever you do or say or create . . . if you *truly* believe it to be art, then it is. At least to the artist.

The ARTIST *takes off his shoes now. Places them carefully next to the* SUBJECT. *Just to one side of him.*

ARTIST And once it's "art," it should be untouchable. Out of reach. Something to look at, to study, to talk about and argue over, even . . . art should elicit *all* of those responses . . . BUT it should also always be given a place of honor and have that place respected. As a work of "art."

The ARTIST *unbuttons his trousers and takes them off. With care he folds them and places them on top of his folded shirt and his coiled belt.*

He points at someone in the audience.

ARTIST . . . who are you to tell me what I do isn't "art?" (*Points at another person.*) Or you? (*To another.*) Or you? I mean, hell . . .

look at you. (*Smiles.*) You're willing to go out in public wearing *that*
. . . why would I ever let you judge what *I* do? I mean, really. *Get*
thee to a Gap store, my friend! Seriously.

The ARTIST *reaches into his underwear and feels his cock. He contin-*
ues to speak as he does this.

ARTIST   But I digress . . .

The ARTIST *removes his hand from his underwear and looks out at the*
audience. Nods and then indicates the SUBJECT.

ARTIST   If I was to do this—what I'm about to do to this subject—
at my home, in the privacy of my own place . . . well then, it'd just
be sex and that'd be that. Now, I *have* given him a pill, a muscle
relaxer . . . to calm his nerves, that is true . . . so maybe you could
argue that it's something else . . . abuse. Assault. Or rape, even.
Yes. "Rape." So many folks love to rush to that judgment when
there is sex involved . . . when there's a man *and* a woman involved, or two guys, even . . . oh yes, they do. But that is not true
in this case. If we'd met at a bar or in school or something like that
then maybe, *maybe* you could call it that if I gave him a pill and
then had my way with him but that is not the case here . . . *no.*
Not at all. (*Points to the* SUBJECT.) He's *fully* aware of what we're
doing here tonight. He has said Yes and given me his okay and
signed a release even. Oh yes, he has. (*Smiles.*) I covered my ass,
don't you worry about that! Have to these days. And so I did.
(*Pointing.*) Do not let that look on his face fool you: this subject
knows EXACTLY what he's gotten himself into. (*Beat.*) Trust me.

The ARTIST *smiles, yawns, and then sniffs his hand several times.*
Reaches over with both hands and pulls down the back of the
SUBJECT'*s pants.*

ARTIST This one's an art student. Studying over there at the university. I think he even gets some credit for doing this . . . extra credit or that kind of thing. Counts as a "work/study" sort of deal, being with a person like me . . . man of my stature. Emerging artist. (*Smiling.*) That MacArthur grant counts for a little something, now, doesn't it? Yes, it sure does . . .

The ARTIST *reaches down and pulls his underwear down and off. Pulls them up to his face in his hands and smells them. Deeply.*

ARTIST Mmmmmmmmmmm. I fucking love "art." Don't you? (*Beat.*) I LOVE it . . .

The ARTIST *reaches over and pulls the tape off the* SUBJECT*'s mouth.*

He starts to protest but the ARTIST *slowly shoves the underwear into his mouth. A bit at a time. Covering his mouth back over with the tape.*

ARTIST HOWEVER: Even artists have to be careful today. To not be silenced . . . to not be accused. (*Smiles.*) To not get sued. All that shit. It's true. (*Beat.*) These are dangerous times, people . . . but hey . . . you know that. (*Beat.*) That's why I do this *exactly* the same way. *Each* time . . . *every* time . . . because that's what makes it ART. Hell, I'm not even *gay* and neither is he, so, I mean . . . it's *gotta* be ART! (*Smiles.*) Right? (*Beat.*) . . . what else you gonna call it, if not that? (*Shrugs.*) You tell me . . .

The ARTIST *points down at the* SUBJECT*'s bare ass. Indicating as he speaks.*

ARTIST This is my canvas. Right here. This soft white flesh. This sweet pink hole . . . this one . . . here. (*Slips a finger inside him.*) Blank. Perfect. Untouched. He's promised me that's the case. That he's never done this before . . . had a man in his ass. And I believe him, from the looks of it. How it feels in there. I don't think he has . . . (*He removes his finger and he tastes it.*) Nope. That's tight. Nice and tight . . .

The ARTIST *stops now, standing there with his cock in his hand and talking to the audience.*

ARTIST Watch me now, ladies and gentlemen, as I paint another portrait in this subject's ass with my cock. Paint his backside with my jizz like Mr. Jackson Pollock before me. I mean, paint. Cum. What does it really it matter . . .? These are simply the tools of the trade. The rest . . . is . . . *semantics.*

The ARTIST *spits on his hand and rubs the saliva up and down his shaft. He puts his cock inside the* SUBJECT. *The* SUBJECT *screams out in a muffled voice as his body is violated.*

ARTIST Listen to that: the sound of my art. Look in his eyes: the effect of my work as I'm creating. It's beautiful, isn't it? Don't you think? (*Beat.*) Two thousand years of Western History played out as metaphor . . . art and politics fighting it out . . . as they are destined to do . . . time and time again. Forever and always.

The ARTIST *shoves his cock in and out of the* SUBJECT. *Back and forth. Holding his ass with his two hands and thrusting. Over and over.*

ARTIST But I digress . . .

The SUBJECT *continues to scream out. His voice muffled by the underwear and the tape.*

ARTIST I can't lie to you . . . I *love* my work. I do. And look at this. The things I make with it. The beauty of my creation. (*He reaches down and touches the* SUBJECT *and his ass. Pulls up two fingers covered in blood.*) That shit is just . . . lovely. No, it's more than that. More than "lovely." This is ART. And why? Because I say so. And I'm an artist. So I should know . . . (*Beat.*) Right?

The ARTIST *wipes his fingers on the* SUBJECT*'s ass and continues. He finally starts to climax and bends his head down. With a final thrust he finishes. Emptying himself inside his subject.*

ARTIST Oh yeah . . . oh yeah . . . oh fuck yes . . . (*He stops and gathers himself.*) Now THAT is a work of art. Right there. (*Pointing.*) That is fucking beautiful. And all the pictures and postcards and entries in magazines and journals will never see it the way that you have . . . all of you here tonight . . . watching me as I worked. As I created. Sitting there and watching me and letting it happen . . . oh yes . . . you know you did.

The ARTIST *pulls his cock out and wipes it on the* SUBJECT*'s ass. Pulls his underwear back up around himself.*

ARTIST There. Always have to sign your work.

The ARTIST *taps the* SUBJECT *on the ass with affection. Leans on him as he finishes talking with us.*

ARTIST So many people've paved the way for me and what I do . . . people banging away on themselves or others . . . cutting themselves up and doing shit to make their point . . . Abramović . . . Emin . . . hell, even Sulkowicz. (*Smiling.*) Bet she got sick of lugging that fucking *mattress* around during the wintertime! Don't you think? On some of those snowy days . . . when it got real cold out? Oh well. Nobody could tell her NO and it was her *right* and that's *free speech* and all that . . . but damn! I bet it sucked . . . right around February or so . . . (*Laughs.*) But she did it. And that's her "art," so God bless. She took a stand. And hey, men have, too, of course. Chris Burden, *obviously*, and dear Steven Cohen, with that little rooster attached to his cock . . . coq-on-coq, they called it. In Paris. And many more . . . folks getting shot dead for drawing a couple pictures of Mohammed . . . I mean . . . that shit is crazy. Right? No matter who you are . . . what church or politics you've got . . . *right*? That is fucking crazy. (*He indicates the* SUBJECT.) Anyway, look. What I've done here is nothing new . . . maybe not even provocative in this day and age . . . but look at him . . . ladies and gentlemen . . . take a long look at him and then try and tell me that what you see before you is not ART . . . (*Beat.*) In fact, I dare you. I defy you to. (*Beat.*) Go on. (*Beat.*) Say it.

The ARTIST *waits. If anyone in the audiences disagrees, the* ARTIST *should say "says you." If no one disagrees, then the* ARTIST *should say "told you so."*

After that he should begin to re-dress himself during the following:

ARTIST   See? That's the beauty of "art." You and I can think the same thing . . . or the exact opposite . . . and we can both be right. But no matter what we feel . . . it has the right to be expressed. To be seen. Experienced. (*Beat.*) ART. (*Beat.*) Doesn't it?

The ARTIST *stops. Smiles. Sniffs his fingers. Taps the* SUBJECT *in front of him affectionately on the ass.*

ARTIST   Thank you for sharing this *opening* with me tonight. (*Beat.*) That's a play on words, by the way . . . for the slower ones out there.

The ARTIST *bows and then straightens up. Smiles. Bows again.*

ARTIST   Enjoy the rest of your evening. (*Smiling.*) Good night.

The ARTIST *turns and walks out. The* SUBJECT *remains. Looking out at us. Silence. Darkness.*

16 POUNDS

16 POUNDS had its world premiere as part of "Mouthful" (a collection of food crisis plays) at Trafalgar Studios in London, England, in September 2015.
It was directed by Poppy Burton-Morgan.

DIDI   Alisha Bailey
GOGO   Robert Hands

Silence. Darkness.

A desk and a swivel chair in a room. Another chair sits in a lighted spot in front of the desk.

A WOMAN *sitting at the desk, dressed in a suit. She looks off into the distance, then stretches her neck and back.*

Pitcher of water on the table. After a moment, she turns and stands up. Pours a glass of water.

She spills a little onto the desk.

DIDI . . . oh, damn.

The WOMAN *leans forward and uses her hand to slide these few drops back down into the glass.*

She sits back down, takes a sip of water from the glass and then sets it on the desk.

After a moment, she hits a button on the desk. Sound of a buzzer overhead and down the hallway. Very loud. After a beat, she speaks into a little box on the desk.

DIDI Next . . .

After a moment, a MAN *enters the room. Timid. Not well-kempt. He stands behind the chair in the lighted spot.*

The WOMAN *at the desk gestures to him.*

DIDI . . . no, no, please. Sit. No need to be so formal. You should sit. (*Beat.*) Go on.

GOGO Thank you.

The MAN *is tentative but finally sits in the chair.*

DIDI Long day, I'm sure . . .

GOGO It was, yes.

DIDI That awful long line. Right? The line to get in here. Up to this place. To see me.

GOGO Yes.

DIDI Terrible. We're trying to do something about that, but as you can imagine . . . lots of people to see. So many people. People like you . . . who want something.

GOGO I understand.

DIDI Of course you do. I mean, you're the one who stood there all day. In the sun. In the heat. Without food. Without drink . . .

GOGO That's right.

DIDI To get here. To speak with me. Isn't that right? (*Beat.*) To talk with me about this.

She points to the glass of water—which he has been looking at almost since he first got into the room.

GOGO Yes.

DIDI No one hurt you, did they? The people outside, the *troops* and all that? Those men out there, with the dogs and guns . . . none of them hurt you in any way, did they?

GOGO . . . no.

DIDI That seems a bit tentative. Be *honest*.

GOGO No one "hurt" me.

DIDI I see. (*Beat.*) But . . .?

GOGO There was some yelling. They're harsh at times. The men. And the dogs. They would get close and scream or let the animals bark at you . . . at times. Or bite. (*Shows his hand*.) One nipped me. Here.

DIDI I see. (*Beat*.) Well, it is a *lot* of people to deal with . . . true? Wouldn't you agree?

GOGO I would. Yes.

DIDI And sometimes . . . it doesn't justify them to be violent or any- thing like that . . . I'm not saying that, *but* . . . it is a great wave of people that we're handling here. A *huge* number of you who want to be here. Who've been given the chance to be here.

GOGO That's true.

DIDI Yes. It is. (*Pointing*.) For this.

The WOMAN *picks up the glass and holds it above the desk. She pours a little onto the top of the desk, where the water pools up on the wooden surface.*

The MAN *sits forward but stops himself. Watching. After a moment he can't help himself and bursts into tears. Just sits there and weeps.*

The WOMAN *sits back in her chair and watches him. Then:*

DIDI Oh, no, don't do that . . .

GOGO I'm sorry.

DIDI Don't cry.

GOGO I can't help it. I just . . .

DIDI That's alright. It's fine. It's just a teensy little spill . . . that's all . . .

GOGO I know. I see that. But . . . I'm . . . I'm . . .

DIDI No, I understand. I do. (*Pointing*.) You can have that. All of it. Right there. (*Pointing again*.) Go ahead. It's alright.

The MAN *looks at her and then, very tentatively, goes to the desk and licks the water up off the surface of it.*

The WOMAN *stands up while he does this. Pats him on the top of the head. Stroking his hair a few times.*

DIDI See? We're not monsters . . .

GOGO Thank you.

He licks the table one more time and then goes back to his chair. She sits again. He and the WOMAN *sit for a long minute without speaking. Silence.*

DIDI Good, right?

GOGO Yes.

DIDI Better than you remember or about the same?

GOGO Even better.

DIDI It always is, isn't it? When you haven't had something for a while and then you're given it again . . . it's even better, right? Better than just the memory of it.

GOGO I think so. (*Beat.*) Yes.

DIDI Oh, I know so. It's scientific. It really is . . . "craving" something . . . that makes it even better when you finally get it.

GOGO . . . that's probably true . . .

DIDI Absolutely true. It *absolutely* is. (*Beat.*) And this is it. What you're looking at is really it. I mean, not the last of it, of course . . . not the *very* end . . . but it is almost done. Our supplies are almost gone and when that happens . . . then yes. We're fucked. We really are. (*Beat.*) *Everybody*.

GOGO That's true . . .

DIDI Uh-huh. I mean, sure, *now* you agree. Of course now you do . . . because it's gone. But did you always feel that way? When things were fine—and by *fine* I mean it just kept spilling out of your tap, each and every time you turned it on? I don't expect you to answer that, by the way . . . I know what the answer is. Of course not! Who did? *No* one. Nobody. (*Beat.*) A few of us did . . . we talked about it, wagged our fingers and went on talk shows and said not just that it *might* happen . . . that it *could* happen . . . we said it *would* happen. (*Holds up her hands.*) And it *did*. (*Beat.*) We ran out. It's gone. Mostly, anyway. Most of our water supply in the world—not just here but everywhere, and I'm saying "*every*where"—it's finished . . . we wasted it. (*Beat.*) And that took some doing, by the way. Not just our endless decades of consumption . . . not just that . . . but climate change —which no one wanted to believe was real . . . okay, well, fine then! I guess because you say so then it's not!—And not even that fully did us in. Not even that. No, first we had to export drought . . . do you know what I mean by that? (*To the* MAN.) Do you?

GOGO   I don't, no. (*Beat.*) Sorry.

DIDI   Of course you don't. You *did* it . . . along with everybody else . . . but you had no idea what the fuck you were doing. (*Beat.*) Same way you did everything else in your life. (*Beat.*) Oh well. Here we are. (*Beat.*) What I mean by that is . . . first we made sure we took all the water from other countries around the world . . . even ones who already were experiencing drought . . . didn't matter to us . . . we still took water from them to use for ourselves. At home. The office. And raising our food. Mostly for that.

GOGO   Oh.

DIDI   Yes. "Oh." Well put. Very well put . . . (*Beat.*) We used tons and tons and tons of water, every day, every single day just to produce a pound or two of beef . . . or chicken . . . or pork. (*Beat.*) TONS of water. Over and over and over. (*Beat.*) And now look at us . . .

GOGO   . . .

DIDI   Exactly. (*Smiles.*) Not much to say about it, is there? No, not now. Not any more.

GOGO   . . .

DIDI   Not all of us, of course . . . some of us planned ahead . . . got wise to the whole thing and saved some—of course we did—or I'd be over there with you now, with my head bowed and answering my annoying questions . . . you're over there in that chair because you were one of the folks who ran the faucet the whole time you were brushing your teeth and taking so many showers—my God, people used to take a *lot* of showers, didn't they?! SO many! (*Laughs.*) Not anymore, though. Right? I mean, look at you. You're filthy. When was the last time you took a shower . . . like a *hot* shower in a proper bathroom? When would that be? (*Beat.*) Seriously. Take a guess. (*Beat.*) Just for fun.

GOGO . . . I can't remember.

DIDI Yes. That's what I hear all the time. None of you can actually remember it . . . and it's probably been what? In reality only a few months or a year or whatever, but when I ask folks—people who come and sit in that very same chair—that's what I usually hear from them. "I can't remember." (*Beat.*) Amazing how it can all go to shit so fucking fast . . . isn't it?

GOGO Yes.

DIDI Well, it amazes me, anyway. It really does. (*Beat.*) One of the great mysteries of mankind, actually . . . how did we get SO good at fucking things up? Fucking them up so completely and so fully that it's impossible to go back and fix 'em again. (*She shrugs.*) I dunno, but we are. We're great at it. The best there is. (*Beat.*) Oh well . . .

The WOMAN *reaches out and takes the glass of water on the desk. Drinks most in one gulp. Tosses the rest aside.*

The MAN *puts his hands to his face—tries to stop himself from crying out. Only partially successful.*

DIDI That's really good. I mean, remember when your parents would tell you how good it was—water, I mean—when you'd want an icy cold Coke or something, middle of a hot summer day and your mum or dad would say "just have a glass of water, it's the most refreshing thing there is" and you'd just hate 'em for it, *hate* 'em for saying such stupid shit to you when you really wanted a Coke or something but now that we're here at this place you realize it was kinda true . . . that water was the best thing we had and completely natural and we had a TON of it . . . I mean, an endless supply . . . or so we thought . . . and now this is it. Here we are. We're fucked. Or, I mean, *you* are. People like you. Not me. Not for now. For a little bit longer I will be in this chair and not that chair, where you're sitting, but who knows? All I know is everything is gonna come to an end, really fast and really soon now and it's no joke and we all used to think it was . . . think the environment and food and water and recycling and the animals and everything was just a huge fucking joke. And then it wasn't . . . and people got very scared and panicked and a lot of people got sick or died or killed themselves and the government stepped in and . . . blah blah-blah . . . and here we are. You there and me here and this is how it goes . . . (*Beat.*) The-end-of-the-world.

The MAN *nods at this, his head still tilted down. Not looking into the eyes of the* WOMAN.

GOGO Yes.

DIDI Yes.

GOGO I know . . .

DIDI I know you know.

GOGO And . . . I'm ashamed . . .

DIDI You should be. Everybody should be. But we weren't. Not enough of us, anyway . . . and not soon enough. We just weren't.

(*Beat.*) We always think there's going to be a "tomorrow." Sun'll come up and the day will happen and so will the next one and the next one and the next one. Like, forever. And we'll have to work hard and plan and save but there will always be things for us. "Things." The basics, at least . . . we'll ALWAYS have the basics . . . food and water and shelter. (*Beat.*) But—as we've seen— that's just not the case.

GOGO That's true.

DIDI It is true.

GOGO I *know*.

DIDI Good.

GOGO Yes. (*Beat.*) I really do know. *Now*.

DIDI Doesn't really mean shit though, now, does it? Since almost everybody on the planet is dying of hunger and thirst . . . but hey . . .

The WOMAN *nods to herself and trails off, thinking about this. The* MAN *is quiet. Keeps his head down.*

DIDI Anyway, you're here today. You braved the line . . . you fought your way through that crowd and you made it inside. In here to see me.

GOGO Yes.

DIDI Yes.

GOGO I did.

DIDI So that's something. (*Beat.*) Was it worth it?

GOGO I'm sorry?

DIDI Doing all that . . . was it worth it? To live on with a little bit of water—what I'm about to give you—to struggle on for a few more days with what you'll take away from here . . . do you feel now that it was worth it? (*Beat.*) I mean, since this will most probably be your last trip through the line . . . since you have nothing left to

trade. To give up. (*Smiles.*) Well . . . your wife, I suppose . . .
(*Smiles.*) Unless she beats you to it. (*Beat.*) So. Was it worth it?

GOGO   . . .

DIDI   That's a hard one, right? That question?

GOGO   . . . yes . . .

DIDI   Yes, I thought so. Most people try to answer it but they just . . .
yep. Kind of trail off the way you did . . . shrug their shoulders
and mumble and . . . you know . . . that's what they say: nothing,
like you did, or "I dunno" sometimes . . . a big fat "I don't know."
Because they don't. At all. They don't really understand how
they could've done what they've done—some of the outrageous
shit that they have done to survive—BUT they've done it. They
thought about it and weighed it out and, in the end, they did it.
To fuel that most basic of all human instincts: to live on. To crawl
forward for another day . . . an hour . . . one tiny little second . . .

GOGO   It's true. (*Beat.*) I've . . . I've done . . . oh my God . . . the
things I've done . . .! GOD!!

The MAN *bursts into tears again. Covers his face with his hands and
shakes his head.*

DIDI   I don't wanna tell you your business but if it was me . . . I'd
be careful with those tears. Water being as scarce as it is . . .

The MAN *nods and forces himself to stop. The* WOMAN *waits for him
to finish. She finally stands and points toward a wall in the room.
Stacks of one gallon containers of water.*

She motions for the MAN *to go to the wall.*

DIDI   It's alright. You can take your water and go. It's fine. No
worries.

The MAN *quietly goes to the wall. Turns back to look at the* WOMAN.

GOGO Yes?

DIDI Yes. (*Beat.*) You get two. As agreed upon when you got into line. Two gallons. Go ahead. (*Beat.*) No one will hurt you . . . at least no more than already's been done. I promise you that. (*Beat.*) *Go* on.

GOGO Thank you.

DIDI You're welcome.

GOGO Thank you . . . thank you . . . thank . . .

DIDI Please, stop. It's alright . . . you earned it, I'm sure.

GOGO Yes.

The MAN *is barely strong enough to carry the two gallons but he manages. Staggering off toward the door.*

The WOMAN *stops him with her voice before he can exit:*

DIDI Before you go, though . . . remind me what you did . . . what you gave up for those two little containers? Those *16* pounds . . .?

GOGO . . .

DIDI I'm sure I could look it up but all these stories run together and I forget how you or this person or that one did what they did . . . for that. (*Pointing.*) So tell me.

GOGO . . .

DIDI Oh, go on. It's just us here. No one else will know. Or care. I promise you . . .

GOGO . . .

DIDI Not with the way things are these days. It doesn't really matter. You did it . . . it's done . . . that's all.

GOGO I've done . . . terrible things . . . (*Starting to cry again.*) My . . . my children . . .

DIDI Yes! That's right! Your daughter, was it? Or maybe your son? Am I remembering that correctly . . .?

GOGO Yes.

DIDI Yes what? Which?

GOGO Both.

DIDI Oh. (*Beat.*) *Both.* (*Beat.*) Both children.

GOGO Yes.

DIDI You gave up *both*?

GOGO Yes. My wife and I . . . *we* . . . we were . . .

DIDI I see. (*Beat.*) For water. (*Beat.*) For a bit of drinking water. For you.

GOGO Yes. (*Beat.*) And my wife.

DIDI For that. (*Pointing.*) Right there. (*Beat.*) For a few *pounds* of water.

GOGO Yes.

DIDI Hmmm. I see. (*Beat.*) Death or pleasure? (*Beat.*) You let them be killed or given to the troops for . . .? (*Beat.*) Which?

GOGO I'm not . . . I think they killed the boy and then . . . they took the girl . . . for . . . the . . .

DIDI Right. (*Beat.*) Fine. (*Beat.*) Well, I hope you and your wife enjoy the water. Really. You should. Every last drop . . .

GOGO Thank you.

DIDI Oh, no, don't thank me . . . *please.*

The MAN *nods and starts off. After a beat, she speaks:*

DIDI You can thank yourselves.

He turns at this thought. Taking it in. The weight of it. He nods and moves quietly out of the room.

The WOMAN *is alone now. She goes to her desk and sits. With a sigh she stretches her back and neck. She's tired.*

Finally she reaches forward and pours another glass of water. Leaves it on the desk.

After a moment, she hits a button on the desk. Sound of a buzzer overhead and down the hallway. Very loud. After a beat, she speaks into a little box on the desk.

DIDI   Next . . .

Silence. Darkness.

BFF

BFF is a stage adaptation of the short film of the same name. The film had its world premiere at the Tribeca Film Festival in New York City in April 2012.
It was directed by Neil LaBute.

JACK   Thomas Sadoski
JILL   Gia Crovatin
JOSH   Chris Henry Coffey

Silence. Darkness.

We plunge right in on two people—coffee mugs on the table in front of them—who are sitting across from each other. Staring. A silence.

She is dressed in office suit and skirt. He's in shorts and a t-shirt. Looks a bit rumpled. Finally, the woman can't take it anymore and blurts out:

JILL   . . . what?

JACK   Nothing.

JILL   No, not nothing, please. You're looking at me like I was . . . some . . .

JACK   I'm not, either . . .

JILL   Yes, you are, yes! You are sitting there with a smile on your face but inside you are saying to yourself "Jesus Christ, my friend is crazy!" You are, you're saying that, I can tell.

JACK   Jill, I'm not. I promise you.

JILL   Fine. I can tell, but fine.

JACK   No, not fine! I'm not trying to . . . what? What's the word?

JILL   I dunno.

JACK   Yes, you do, it's . . . shit! Come on. What's the word for what you think I'm trying to do to you but I'm—placate! I'm not trying to *placate* you. That's the thing I am *not* doing here! Is that.

JILL   Ok, so, you're just what then? Amused at me? *Bemused*? Which is it? I'm never sure with those two words.

JACK   I don't know—I think they both apply at this point, actually.

JILL Really? They do?

JACK Kinda. Yeah. (*Beat.*) You're being a little nuts about this. Showing up here right in the middle of the . . . you know . . .

JILL It's my break time! I can use it however I want to!

JACK I know that, I *know,* I'm just saying . . . I'm in the shower and you're out there banging on the . . . wham, wham, wham!

JILL What? This is important to me! He's my *boyfriend*!

JACK Jill, I get it, I understand that, that's not what I'm saying— it's the *approach* . . .

JILL Well, how should I approach it? Huh? Just ask him, maybe at dinner tonight: "Honey, are you fucking somebody? Are you banging the shit outta some woman at your office or am I just being silly?" Maybe approach it like that? Would that work?

JACK No! Obviously not, Jesus, that's not what I mean . . . of course not.

JILL Then what?

JACK I don't know! I'm not a . . . I'm your friend here, not some . . . some . . .

JILL You are my BFF, Jack, my *B-F-F.* We have shared *every*thing since college—I even moved here 'cause of you—and that's why I'm here now, begging for your help. I'm desperate! I love this fucking guy . . .

JACK I know you do, and that's why you should maybe just . . . step back for a . . .

JILL I can't! You know what I found, what I've started to notice in the last few—he's not being honest with me! He is seeing somebody and I need to act here. Right now!

JACK Fine.

JILL Sorry but I do.

JACK I said "fine." Ok. So . . . hire someone.

JILL   *Hire*? (*Beat.*) You mean, like . . . what? One of those girls who try to catch him out or, or, or . . . that kinda thing? I thought that was just on TV.

JACK   No, people do that.

JILL   Really?

JACK   Yeah, but that's not what I'm . . .

JILL   *Seriously*?

JACK   Yes, but I'm talking about a guy, not some lady, but a *man* who—a detective.

JILL   Oh. So you're saying like a . . . *real* . . .?

JACK   I mean, yeah. Yes. If you need that. An investigator, or some other . . . type . . .

JILL   That'd be . . . I mean, I guess I could . . .

JACK   Happens all the time.

JILL   I know, I'm sure, it's just . . . (*Beat.*) Wait! Wait, you could do it for me!

JACK   What?! No—are you insane?! NO FUCKING WAY! *EVER*!

JILL   Why? Why not?!

JACK   *Because* I'm not gonna get—Jill, no!! Absolutely not. Stop.

JILL   Fine. (*Beat.*) So where would I find some person like that, then? Where?

JACK   I don't know! You're acting like I have—what about online? Some guy who follows him . . . reports back to you and all that shit. Like people did in the olden days.

JILL   Yeah . . . that's possible. I guess.

JACK   You haven't done anything like that yet, have you? Had him trailed, or, or . . .?

JILL   No, of course not! This just started, I told you.

JACK   Right, that's right . . .

JILL   I saw that shirt of his there, the one he crunched down in the hamper and I pulled it out and smelled it . . . I did, sniffed it and it reeked of *sex*. You know how it is when you get a whiff of that? It's just, like . . . *un*-deniable. Anyway, that started me thinking about, you know . . . a lot of other behavior. He's later and later at work . . . sometimes out when he says he'll be in at the office, dinners and all that crap. It adds up!

JACK No, I get it. I get what you're . . . (*Beat.*) And you can't just . . . ask him?

JILL What's he gonna say?

JACK Well, I mean . . . maybe he'll . . .

JILL He's a *man*! This is his *profession*—liar! No offense, but . . .

JACK Ha! True, but, still—if you guys have any kind of real relationship he might wanna talk with you about it . . . get it out . . . maybe it's killing him and he's just on the edge, hoping you'll find out. *Maybe* he's actually putting it out there so you will confront him about it. Just so he's able to start the conversation . . .

JILL So you think he *is* doing it! Fuck!

JACK No, I'm not saying that! Stop now, stop it! (*Beat.*) I'm *saying* that if this crap is true then you need to do something . . .

JILL Well, God, I know that . . . but what? *What*?!

JACK I don't know! You're always going on and on about how great you guys are together and blah-blah-blah, so just ask him then. Point-blank.

JILL That's not . . . I can't! What if it's not happening and I ruin everything? Or even worse . . . if I put the idea in his head?!

JACK . . . it's . . . the risk you take . . .

JILL Maybe I could . . . what if I found a *hair* or something . . . what about DNA tests or some deal like that?

JACK Please! Is that realistic?

JILL   I don't know! They do it on *CSI*! At least on the *Miami* one,
I don't watch the other ones . . .

JACK   Come on, you're being . . . (*Beat.*) Shit. I'm so gonna regret—
do you *really* want me to follow him, after work or something, for
a few weeks? Do you?

JILL   Oh, God . . . I mean . . . you'd do that? Really?

JACK   For you I would. We're BFFs. (*Beat.*) I'd have to be careful . . .
he knows me so it could be such a bad, stupid thing if we get
caught but yeah, I'd do that for you. Of course.

JILL   Wow, I don't know what to say . . .

JACK   I just want you to think about it and to be sure you know
what you're doing. This is *such* dangerous territory here—this'd
be me *tailing* him once he gets off work until he comes home to
you. It's serious stuff . . .

JILL   . . . no, I get that . . .

JACK   You're saying that you don't trust the man you supposedly
love. A guy you've told me you wanna marry . . .

JILL   I do! I want to. But . . .

JACK   But you think he's with somebody and it's eating you alive.
Right? I can see that.

JILL   It is. It *really* is. (*Eyes well up.*) Can't fucking sleep—I just
lay there at night, staring at him . . . hour after hour. Wondering.
I'm going through his phone numbers and emails, shit I know
would make him go *ballistic* if he found me out but I can't help
it! I literally can't help myself as I'm doing it. It's killing me,
Jack . . .

JACK   . . . it's ok . . .

JACK *picks up the coffee mugs and moves them into the kitchen.
Drops them into the sink as* JILL *watches him intently. Waiting.*

JILL I know you haven't had one of these long-term things for
a while so it doesn't feel the same to you, but trust me . . .

JACK . . . hey, I've had a few . . . that's not true! People who wanted
to, you know . . . be my . . .

JILL No, I'm not saying . . . you know what I mean by that, though.
Right?

JACK . . . yeah. No, I get it. I'm just . . .

JILL And even if you did—had a relationship right now, I mean—
you're *stronger* than I am. You've always been a tougher person
than me, Jack . . .

JACK That's true.

JILL So . . .

JACK Yeah. So, so, so. (*Beat.*) Anyway . . .

JILL Yes. Anyway. I need to get back. I said I was just running out to
Starbucks!

JACK Ha! You wanna get outta here so you can try and catch him
out at lunch, *that's* why you need to get going . . . right?

JILL No . . .

JACK Come on, be honest!

JACK *presses her with a look and finally* JILL *gives in with a smile.
Shakes her head to the affirmative.*

JILL Yes, ok! (*Laughs.*) I might run over there and just see if he's—
said he was gonna be at Cubby's down there on Sixth, that sports
bar, so I thought as long as I'm on my way back that I'd . . .

JACK *Jill.* (*Beat.*) Just be careful. Ok?

JILL Of what?

JACK Getting what you wish for.

JILL . . . I know. God, you're so smart! Always have been.

JACK Not true, I just care about you. That's all.

JILL Love you.

JACK Me too. My BFF.

JILL Ha! Ok, gotta run . . .

JACK Seriously? Don't go by there right now—it'll ruin your day.
Even if he's there, and I'm sure he is, he'll be talking to some
female exec or something and you'll misread it and be all pissed
during the afternoon . . . just head back to work, grab a sandwich,
and I promise to start in tonight. I'll go over there at five.

JILL He's supposedly going to the *gym* after work.

JACK Then I'll watch him do it. I'll text you if he puts a foot wrong.

JILL Yeah?

JACK You know I will. If he's got a girl on the side, you're gonna be
the first to know about it.

JILL Thanks, sweetie.

JACK Of course! Hey, you'd do the same for me, right? (*Smiles.*)
I mean, if I was seeing somebody long enough for them to cheat
on me, that is!

JILL I didn't mean anything by that.

JACK I'm kidding! Now go.

JILL Love you. My BFF.

JACK You, too.

JILL *gets up and walks to the door.* JACK *follows her and lets her out.
He locks the door and goes to the kitchen.*

*He starts to wash the two coffee cups, picking them up from the sink.
From the other room comes a male voice.*

VOICE (O.S.) . . . she gone?

JACK Yep.

A bedroom door opens and a good-looking guy stands in the open-

ing. Wearing just his boxers. This is JILL*'s* GUY*, who has been waiting patiently to finish his "lunch." His name is* JOSH.

JOSH Jesus. I thought she was gonna move in!

JACK Me, too! (*Beat.*) I heard that first knock and I knew it was her, you know? I mean, I just *knew* it! You're laying there, all ready to cum and of course she shows up: she's like a fucking *Rolex* . . .

JOSH Ha! Think she's gonna go by the bar?

JACK Of course she is! She's gonna call me in about twenty minutes. I promise you.

JOSH *Great.* What should I say when I see her tonight?

JACK I have no idea. That's your problem.

JOSH Thanks, dude. (*Beat.*) And watch it with my shirts, would ya? Keep your stink off me! (*Beat.*) I mean, what the hell am I gonna say to her now that she's going through my *laundry* and shit?! I mean . . .

JACK Ha! You'll think of something—you always do.

JOSH True.

JACK Tell ya what: You can work on your speech while I'm sucking your cock. (*Beat.*) How's that for fair?

JOSH I think that's more than fair . . .

JACK Well, good, 'cause I wanna be fair. (*Smiles.*) She is my BFF, after all.

JOSH . . . since college, apparently . . .

JACK That's absolutely right. (*Beat.*) And like she said: we share *every*-thing.

They smile that wicked smile that comes with deception as together they entwine and retreat into the bedroom.

We watch them through the doorway for a moment. Fucking.

Silence. Darkness.

BLACK GIRLS

BLACK GIRLS had its world premiere as part of "NY Madness" at Atlantic Theater Company, Atlantic Stage 2 in New York City in September 2015.

It was directed by Marco Calvani.

GIRL   Shayna Small
GUY   John Concado

Silence. Darkness.

Two people sitting on a bench. Staring out. WHITE GUY *and a* BLACK GIRL. *Just so you know.*

GIRL   . . . so. It's "No," then. (*Beat.*) Right?

GUY   Ummmmmmmmmmmmm . . . yeah, it is, but . . .

GIRL   You won't go with me? To the thingie? That's what you're saying . . .

GUY   I guess. (*Beat.*) Yes. (*Beat.*) I mean "No." (*Beat.*) But . . . to be fair . . . I really don't wanna go to the office party, anyway . . . (*Beat.*) It's not just you.

GIRL   But if you did . . . if you had wanted to go or maybe decide later that you will go . . . you're saying you *don't* want to do that with me. (*Beat.*) Correct?

GUY   Ummmmm . . . yeah. (*Beat.*) I'm sort of saying that . . . but not in a mean way. I'm just saying it like *I'd rather not if that's okay.* (*Beat.*) If it's all the same to you.

GIRL   Well . . . that's . . . it's not really okay . . .

GUY   Oh.

GIRL   It hurts my feelings. (*Beat.*) A lot.

GUY   I know, I can see that, but . . . that's not what I'm trying to do here . . . I am being honest with you, that's all I'm doing . . . (*Beat.*) We don't really know each other that well . . . outside of work, I mean.

GIRL   I see.

GUY   So you should be glad about this. That I'm not lying to you and hiding how I really feel about you . . . or . . . you know . . .

GIRL And how is that? How do you *really* feel about me?

GUY Ummmmmmmmmm . . . you're nice . . . you know? I mean, "very" nice. I'd say.

GIRL "Nice."

GUY Very nice. That's what I said. "Very."

GIRL Okay. (*Beat.*) I'm "very nice." (*Beat.*) And nothing else . . .?

GUY Well, I've always liked working with you, I will say that. You're good to work with and that's important . . . *really* important.

GIRL Great. (*Beat.*) Do you know how hard it was for me to ask you this? About the party? How long it took me to work up to it . . .?

GUY Ummmmmmm . . . no . . . I guess I don't . . .

GIRL On top of all the time I've sat around . . . just hoping that you'd ask me out . . . then I finally get up the courage to see if we could do something together—some simple little thing like the office party—and you say *No.* You don't think about it, or get back to me . . . it's just flat out "NO."

GUY Yeah. I'm sorry . . . but . . . that's . . .

GIRL Is there someone else? In your life?

GUY Ummmmmmmmmmm . . . no, not at the moment.

GIRL Okay, so . . . "NO," then . . . it's not that. (*Beat.*) Is it black women in general . . .? Do you have a problem with us and that's what this is all about? "Women of color?"

GUY No! God, not at all . . . that's not . . . no . . . (*Beat.*) I don't.

GIRL Yeah? You *sure*?

GUY Absolutely not! Please don't say that or, you know . . . spread a rumor about me that's not true. (*Beat.*) I don't feel that way . . .

GIRL Have you ever dated a black woman?

GUY Ummmmmmmmmmm . . . no. I haven't.

GIRL But you like them? I mean, the way they look . . . and . . .?

GUY I haven't really thought about it much . . . but no, I have no problem with them as . . . you know . . . people. Or women. Or whatever.

GIRL *But . . .?*

GUY As I said . . . no . . . I haven't dated one. Up to this point. (*Beat.*) Not yet.

GIRL "Not yet." Is there something that you don't like about us . . . or our looks . . .?

GUY No. Not at all. Not generally, or . . . you know . . . and I think you're *very* . . . I guess I just have a "type." Or something.

GIRL You do? You have a *type*?

GUY I guess. (*Beat.*) Yes. (*Beat.*) Blondes.

GIRL Black girls can go blonde.

GUY Yeah, but it's not . . . that's fake. Dyed, or whatnot. Not like an actual blonde.

GIRL True. (*Beat.*) Okay, so you like blondes, then. But *real* blondes . . . right?

GUY I guess so. Yes.

GIRL So, very pale . . . pale skin and real blonde hair . . . blue eyes, probably?

GUY Yeah. I like that. Green's okay, too . . . or even . . . what's the other one . . .?

GIRL Brown? Like mine?

GUY No . . . more like . . . there's another word for it . . . when they're a mix . . . but like . . .

GIRL *Hazel*?

GUY Yeah! That's it. Hazel. I don't mind that even . . .

GIRL Huh. (*Beat.*) But not brown?

GUY Not my favorite.

GIRL Got it. (*Beat.*) Not brown. (*Beat.*) And what about hair? Like . . . my hair?

GUY What about it? (*Checking phone.*) I need to get back soon . . .
lunch is almost . . .

GIRL I'm just asking. (*Beat.*) Do you like my hair? Or if it was *blonde*
. . . would you like it then, or do you usually like it straighter . . .
not curly, like mine is?

GUY Straighter, I suppose. If I was to . . .

GIRL What?

GUY I don't really even think about all that stuff . . .! (*Beat.*) Not very
often.

GIRL Well, that's not really true now, is it? You've thought about the
way I look . . . and you've decided that it's not for you . . . isn't
that right? That I'm not your type or something like that . . .

GUY I didn't say it that way! *You* pushed me into answering all those
. . . I said I have a *type*. When I am dating . . . I often . . . or almost
always . . . I date the same kind of girl. (*Beat.*) That's not a *crime*,
is it?

GIRL I don't know. Is it? (*Beat.*) I'm asking.

GUY You're not . . . look, I don't wanna do this, what you're doing
here . . . you cornered me today, on my lunch hour . . . asking me
about women and . . . you know . . . their *hair* and . . . *eyes* . . .
and I don't wanna do this sorta thing with you . . . I don't like it.
Please. (*Beat.*) I don't want to go to that office party with you . . .
I'm sorry but I don't . . . people read all sorts of things into who
comes with whom or goes home with whom and what you wear
or how many drinks you have . . . all kinds of crap! You spend the
rest of your year living that stuff down and so . . . no, thank you
. . . if it's alright I'd just rather not do that again . . . so I am being
totally frank and open with you and I hope that you accept that
and we don't have a weird thing between us now. (*Beat.*) Is that
enough? Did I explain it alright . . . or . . . just . . .?

GIRL So . . . you don't want to have to spend the rest of the year living down or explaining your going to the party with *me* . . .? (*Beat.*) Did I understand that correctly?

GUY Oh God! NO! That's not what I said . . . that is NOT what I said when I just said all that stuff . . . a second ago . . . it's NOT . . . (*Beat.*) You're *slanting* what I said.

GIRL But in a way you did say that . . . you said those very words . . . just now. To me.

GUY No, no, no . . . what I said was . . . or *meant* to say, at least . . . was . . . that . . . I'm . . .

GIRL How about my features . . . a black woman's features . . . do you find them attractive? (*Beat.*) Do you think *I'm* pretty?

GUY Oh, for Heaven's sake! Come on!!

GIRL Just tell me . . .

GUY Ok, ok, I will, because otherwise you'll just keep . . . yes. You are. Just not to *me*.

GIRL *Why*? My lips? You don't like full lips?

GUY I do . . . I mean . . . full is nice . . . but not exactly . . . like yours. (*Beat.*) No.

GIRL Why not?

GUY They're . . . too full. Puffy. And with all of that lipstick that you guys use . . .

GIRL "You guys?"

GUY In general! Not *all* black girls always . . . obviously not . . . but yeah, a *lot* of you . . .

GIRL Ok. (*Beat.*) Ok. (*Beat.*) And my nose? Do you like that, or . . . is it . . .?

GUY No. Not really.

GIRL Why? (*Beat.*) Go *on,* you can say it . . .

GUY It's . . . you know . . . I like a *finer* . . . sort of . . . more delicate . . .

GIRL What?

GUY It's thick. Kind of. Your nose.

GIRL I see.

GUY Just for my taste, though . . .

GIRL For *your* taste. Got it . . . (*Beat.*) And my body? Anything else about it that you like or don't like? (*Beat.*) My ass?

GUY Jesus . . . ummmmmmmmmmmmmm . . . it's big . . . I mean . . . you know . . . if I had to say something about it, then I'd say it was big.

GIRL Is that good or bad?

GUY It's *fine*. I'm sure lots of guys like it.

GIRL But is it a "good" or "bad" fine? To *you*?

GUY It's "big!" That's all. Your rear-end is kind of big and, and soft . . . and that's . . .

GIRL Too big? Is it TOO big? (*Beat.*) Tell me! Tell me!! TELL ME!!

GUY For what *I* prefer! *Yes!* I tend to like slimmer girls. Blonde, blue-eyed slim girls and that's just me. It's *not* a racist thing . . . like you're implying . . . it's not. It's just my *personal* choice . . .

He stops for a moment, but he is on a tear now. Wild.

I mean . . . yeah! If you really wanna know! (*Beat.*) And I don't really like your feet, either . . . the way your nails look after they get painted, I don't like that. I think they look like elephant toes and when you sweat, it's different than the way other girls smell, so that's . . . and the way you treat your kids—not *all* of you, of course—but a *lot* of you . . . more than just a few. (*Beat.*) I have seen you slap your own children . . . hard . . . in the face and in public . . . and I do *not* like that. (*Beat.*) It's maybe a social thing and accepted where you come from—not *Africa,* I don't mean that—I'm saying wherever you grew up in America and I don't know, maybe it's like a *cultural* thing, but not here. We don't do that here . . . it's not acceptable. It's *not*.

GIRL Huh.

GUY So . . . that's . . . I don't even know why I said all that, but . . . (*Beat.*) I gotta go.

GIRL I don't have any children.

GUY *Good.* I mean . . . then I wasn't talking to you, obviously. I was not including you in the people I was talking about . . . so just forget that I said anything . . . but that's a pet peeve and it just slipped out because you were . . . *pushing* me . . .

GIRL Yes, but, who're you talking about? (*Beat.*) *Who*? WHO?!

GUY *Other* people! Women I've seen out with their kids . . . like, you know . . . just . . . food stamp people. *That* kind of person. (*Beat.*) You *know* who I mean . . .! You *do*! Those black girls who get all up in the face of anybody who says something to them about child care . . . or . . . you know . . . who can't listen to *reason* about things. Who have kids at 14 and live off of whatever . . . and . . . (*Beat.*) Nothing. Forget it.

GIRL Oh. (*Beat.*) Okay. (*Beat.*) Wow.

GUY I'm going back in now. (*Beat.*) Alright?

GIRL Yes . . . maybe you should . . .

GUY Fine. (*Beat.*) Sorry if that was . . . hell, I dunno. If I was . . . *too* . . .

GIRL *Honest*?

GUY Yeah. Or whatever. Whatever I was . . .

GIRL No, no. I'm glad you were. I appreciate your honesty . . .

GUY Look, I just wanna be . . . to have everything out in the open between us . . .

GIRL It is. I think it absolutely is now.

GUY So we can go back to like it was before.

GIRL *Before*.

GUY   Us. (*Smiles.*) Just co-workers. Side by side. Without all the . . .
you know . . .

GIRL   Uh-huh.

GUY   And not have to worry about this other stuff. (*Beat.*) The
"man/woman" stuff.

GIRL   Got it. (*Beat.*) No, I get it . . .

*She doesn't say anything else as he waits for her. After a moment, he
gathers his things and stands up.*

GUY   Good. (*Beat.*) I hope it's okay about the party and all that . . .
us not going there as a . . . you know . . . some *couple* . . .

GIRL   Yeah, it's okay. (*Beat.*) Trust me. (*Beat.*) I am *very very* okay
with that at this point . . .

GUY   Good.

GIRL   Yes.

GUY   Cool. (*Beat.*) See you black inside, then . . . I mean "black"
. . . "back" . . . "back" inside. I will see you BACK inside, okay?
(*Beat.*) *'Kay*? (*Flustered.*) And no hard feelings . . .

GIRL   Yep. (*Beat.*) 'Bye.

GUY   Okay. (*Beat.*) G'bye.

GIRL   'Bye.

The GUY *leaves and the* GIRL *is left alone. She starts to get up but sits
back down.*

GIRL   . . . no hard feelings.

*She is about to say something else but can't seem to form the right
words. Her bottom lip continues to tremble.*

Silence. Darkness.

SOME WHITE CHICK

SOME WHITE CHICK had its world premiere as part of the "TERROR!" festival at Southwark Playhouse in London, England, in October 2009. It was directed by Jason Lawson.

BRENT   Matthew Stathers
BRIAN   Michael Cox
CHICK   Lucy Caplin

Silence. Darkness.

After a moment, the gloom lifts a bit and we can sense a young man sitting at a table. He's watching something—the shrill sound of screams can be heard coming out of his computer's tiny speakers. He chuckles. Hits a button and the shrieks begin again. He laughs. This is BRIAN.

Something in the corner under a tarp. Moving on occasion.

BRIAN *finally stops what he's doing and goes back to work on a project—he seems to be editing on his Mac. A flurry of different noises, then typing, then noises again.*

A door opens in a wall somewhere and another young man—they're both college-aged—enters. This is BRENT *and he is carrying his backpack and groceries.*

BRENT   . . . hey fucker.

BRIAN   Dude. What's up?

BRENT   Nothing. Cold out there.

BRIAN   Yeah?

BRENT   Uh-huh. I mean, for September . . .

BRIAN   Right.

BRENT   We're gonna get the big, you know, Indian summer and shit soon but right now? 'S a cold one!

BRIAN   'S okay in here, though.

BRENT   Yeah, sure, because we're *underground*. That's why . . .

BRIAN Oh. Yeah.

BRENT Know what I mean?

BRIAN Yep.

BRENT You stay underground when it's cold you got a better chance of staying warm. It's like hibernating.

BRIAN Right. (*Beat.*) . . . I thought heat rises.

BRENT Nope.

BRIAN Really?

BRENT Not when it comes to this. Seriously . . . right here is what the animals do. They burrow into their lairs and stay warm.

BRIAN I guess so. (*Beat.*) You see anything in the papers, or . . .?

BRENT Nope.

BRIAN *Nothing*?

BRENT Or on the news. I checked the locals *and* CNN. They're talking about "some white chick" is all. Not even the lead story around here.

BRIAN Cool.

BRENT *starts to unpack—groceries piling up on the table.*

BRENT I got those chocolate things you like . . . they only had, like, two packs left so I snagged 'em both for you.

BRIAN Thanks, bro.

BRENT *nods, then continues unpacking.* BRIAN *goes back to his typing. After a minute:*

BRIAN Dude, is that true, about the animals and all their hibernating? Is it?

BRENT Yep. I mean, except for, like, dogs and cats and shit. Animals that decide to go live with people, then it's whatever.

BRIAN That's true—they only sleep like we do. Or during the day . . . I mean, if you leave 'em out at night and then they come in first

thing in the morning, all cold and pissed off . . . then they sleep
that day.

BRENT Uh-huh—after they take a shit on the rug or something like
that, though, right?! (*He simulates taking a dump while doing his dog
impression.*) "Thanks a lot for locking the dog door there, buddy!"

BRIAN Ha!

BRENT You know what I'm talking about! (*Beat.*) Pets totally get
back at you for anything you do to them—I've seen it thousands
of times . . .

BRIAN That's funny.

BRENT And true. It's both funny and true.

BRIAN I s'ppose it is.

BRENT *Totally* true. (*Beat.*) Fuck, I've had dogs—this Great Dane
when I was a kid—held a grudge for maybe a month one time.
My mom kicked the thing for chasing skunks near our house, it
was always stinking itself up by doing that, and my mom just
caught it upside the head with her shoe on this one occasion,
smack!, and I swear that fucker just sulked and waited and took
his time and then once, when my mother slipped in her socks on
the wood floors we had there in the house? She slid down to her
knees and that dog lunged at her, ripped a piece of her blouse
and nipped her skin—tore enough of her arm open to go get one
of those tetanus shots—and then he took off running. He knew
exactly what he'd done. And why. Not my mom, obviously, but
the dog. (*Beat.*) How's that for crazy?

BRIAN Wow.

BRENT Yeah. That's right. "Wow." (*Beat.*) Fucking step-dad shot it
the next morning, but for that 24-hour period there where it was
still alive? No question that the dog had been carrying a grudge
around . . .

BRIAN Amazing.

BRENT Not so much. I mean, not really. Stuff like that was always happening when I was a kid. Seems like it, anyway. Don't remember ever having animals around too long at our place. They would get hit by a car or, you know, having to get rid of kittens and all that —that was the worst, dude. Throwing 'em in the pond and shit? Fucking step-dad always made me do it and I hated him for that— I mean, for lots of stuff, but especially that. (*Beat.*) Prick.

BRIAN Huh.

BRENT *picks up the bags that he'd set down on the ground to tell the "dog" story. Moves to another side table in the darkened room.*

BRENT I got chips, so you don't have to ask . . .

BRIAN Sweet! Thanks, man.

BRENT No problem. And dip.

BRIAN Awesome. Mild or Jalepeño?

BRENT I got the Mild—it's all they had.

BRIAN Ok. (*Beat.*) I like the other one, but . . .

BRENT I know, dude! It's *all* they had. It's a market, ok, not like *Safeway* or that kind of deal. (*Beat.*) We're out in the *woods* . . .

BRIAN I know.

BRENT They have, like, *two* selections. You like French Onion? Huh?

BRIAN No. That shit's gay . . .

BRENT Ok then. I got "Mild." It's still cheese.

BRIAN Right. (*Smiles.*) Or whatever they put in there . . .

They laugh at this, gradually getting into some shoving which leads to a bout of boyish wrestling. All smiles.

BRENT Exactly! I don't even know why you like that shit.

BRIAN 'Cause it tastes good. The spicy one is bettter, but . . .

BRENT Faggot, stop! They-didn't-have-it. Okay? I got this one instead.

BRIAN I'm just kidding you . . .

BRENT Fine, then.

BRIAN I like either one. Cheese is cheese . . .

BRENT Pretty much. Except when it's *plastic,* like this shit . . .

BRIAN Ha! Right. (*Beat.*) Else you get?

BRENT You know, just supplies. Meats and a few rolls and stuff. For sandwiches. More of the drinks we both like, shit like that.

BRIAN Cool.

BRENT Enough for the weekend.

BRIAN Nice. Red Bull, too?

BRENT Oh yeah . . . (*Holds something up.*) Oh, and this. Look at this.

BRIAN Mmmmmm. Pie.

BRENT Yep. (*Turns to look at the tarp.*) Hey, hey! Shut up!!

BRENT *goes to the tarp and uncovers a naked and bloody* GIRL. *In her teens. Her mouth is covered and she is tied. He puts a finger to his lips, then removes her gag.*

(*For the rest of the play, the* GIRL *should cry and moan and beg. Stuff like "please" and "help me" and that kind of thing. It should continue to escalate throughout.*)

BRIAN You're gonna be sorry . . .

BRENT I know, but . . .

BRIAN She's not gonna shut up. I promise. Tried it already.

BRENT What's the use of having her here if we can't look at her? I mean . . . (*To her.*) You take it easy, ok? Shhhhh!

BRIAN Yeah, that oughta do it . . .

BRENT Fuck off, bitch! (*Laughs.*) Let's just try.

BRIAN I'm telling you . . . I ended up kicking her in the ribs about *sixty* times. That did it finally.

BRENT Ha! It oughta. (*Simulates kicking a bunch of times.*) Yeah, that should work!

This makes them both giggle. The GIRL *continues to moan.*

BRIAN Kind?

BRENT *What*?

BRIAN Of pie? Kind you get?

BRENT Oh. Mixed berry or some crap.

BRIAN Yum.

BRENT Blueberries and raspberries, but the big ones, too. What're they called?

BRIAN I dunno.

BRENT Of course you don't . . . dumb shit.

BRIAN Hey, that's not . . .

BRENT Kidding. Fucker. (*Thinks.*) You *know* the ones . . .

BRIAN . . . no . . .

BRENT *stops and thinks, sucking on his bottom lip as he does.*

BRENT With the . . . fucking . . . you know! (*Making a gesture.*) Blackberries! That's what they are. They're blackberries.

BRIAN Oh, yeah. 'Course. Blackberries.

BRENT Ha! You didn't know . . .

BRIAN I thought it was something hard. Not so obvious like that. "Blackberries."

BRENT Whatever.

BRIAN Seriously! Those are *local* . . .

BRENT Anyway, it's got 'em in there. For later.

BRIAN That rocks, dude. Should be tasty . . .

BRENT Yep.

BRIAN Nice.

BRENT That's the way we roll . . . getting us the good stuff! Oh yeah.

BRENT *puts the pie on the table along with all the other items that he's purchased.* BRIAN *goes back to his laptop.*

BRENT What're you watching?

BRIAN Yesterday's.

BRENT How is it?

BRIAN It's cool. I added a few little touches.

BRENT What?

BRIAN Not much, don't worry. Just a few bits of sound and stuff, nothing major—that one email asked for more *horror* so I just . . .

BRENT Without me?

BRIAN No—I mean, yeah, I did it while you were outside, not technically "here" but it's not like I was gonna download it or like that until you took a look . . . or . . .

BRENT "Took a look," huh?

BRIAN You know what I mean! Approved it or . . . you *know*.

BRENT Yeah, I do, I know, but do you? Hmmm? Do you understand that I need to see all of it before we put it out there? I thought I was pretty clear about that before . . .

BRIAN Dude, chill.

BRENT No, you chill, dude! Fuck that.

BRIAN It's a couple *sounds* . . . a little creak here or there. That kind of thing.

BRENT Fine.

BRIAN Some water-dripping.

BRENT Good.

BRIAN Same sort of shit we've done before—to the other episodes, so I didn't think . . .

BRENT I'm just saying . . . not-without-me. It's my idea, my *business,* ok, so what I say goes or else. Right? (*Beat.*) RIGHT?

BRIAN Fine.

BRENT Alright. It's important.

BRIAN Got it.

BRENT Great.

BRIAN I-get-it.

BRENT Cool, then let's drop it. Then.

BRIAN Ok by me.

BRENT People want it to be real—they're not gonna pay us for fake shit. 'Kay? It's got to be *real*. They will pay out the nose for anything extra, anything they can't get off TV or the movies or by going in a chat room. Sneaking off to some massage parlor. You know how many times a guy has wanted to strangle the bitch who just gave him head? Probably *three* outa five. Seriously. But do they do it? No, they do not, 'cause they don't wanna go to *prison* . . . but they still *want* to. That's a *fact*. So if they can watch it, I mean, really see it happen, that's the next best thing. That's *us*. And that is what we're doing here. Making dreams come true . . . (*Beat.*) They want fake, all they gotta do is turn on *Cinemax*.

BRIAN Dude, ok, I get it! Jesus . . .

BRENT Ok, fine, so then don't be doing any . . .

BRIAN We did it before!

BRENT When you couldn't hear that one chick's voice! So we added some screams . . . that's all. *Screams*. They were hers, anyways . . .

BRIAN Fine.

BRENT Right?

BRIAN Yeah.

BRENT Good then. (*Beat.*) Look, I'm just saying that the guys who come to us for this shit want a good, clean show is all . . . not any old stuff you can find over on *YouTube*. Right? We're not doing one of those fucking what're-they-called? You know . . . *webisodes* or whatever. They want it to be nasty and they want it to be real. *Private* and real. That's all . . . (*Beat.*) Guy doesn't wanna go through, like, three hundred security questions just to watch some chick go "Ohh, Ohh, Ohh . . ." (*Acting it out.*) Man's paying for hard-core entertainment he wants, like, "Awww! Awwwww! AWWWWWWWW!!!! YOU FUCKING CUNT, AWWWWWW!!!!" (*Acting it out again, this time in manical fashion.*) You know? We want that cash stacking up in our PayPal account we need to know what the fuck we're doing. Ok? At *all* times.

BRIAN Got it.

BRENT 'Kay?

BRIAN Sorry. Fuck.

BRENT Not a problem. I know you were trying to do something positive, but I can't have you messing around with the reality of the thing . . . (*Points.*) Let's have some of that pie, dude. I'm starved.

BRIAN Yeah.

They sit down at the table and stare at the pie. BRENT *looks around, then reaches into his pocket for a knife. He starts in on the dessert, cutting it carefully with the small blade.*

The GIRL *has reached her begging climax, crying out and reaching toward the boys. Pathetic and annoying.*

BRENT AHHHHHH! SHUT UP! SHUT UP!! SHUT THE FUCK UP!!!

Suddenly and without warning, BRENT *jumps up and flies across the room. Landing hard on the* GIRL. *Screaming as he plunges the blade through the tarp, over and over and over again.*

Blood pours out as she dies. Screaming. BRENT *does not stop for some time after this.* BRIAN *stands, watching this. Wide-eyed.*

Silence.

BRIAN   . . . dude.

BRENT   Sorry. Fuck!

BRIAN   Whoa.

BRENT   I know. That wasn't cool . . .

BRIAN   . . . I mean . . .

BRENT *stands, wiping the bloody blade onto his jeans.*

BRENT   . . . but I was trying to have my pie and . . . you know . . . she just wouldn't stop! Shit.

BRIAN   Yeah. (*Beat.*) . . . I didn't even get to film it, though. You coulda *warned* me . . .

BRENT   I know! Damn it!

BRIAN   You were, like, all, bam! Fucking *Bourne Identity* on her ass . . .

BRENT   Ok, shut up! I-get-it. (*Beat.*) Alright, so think, think. Think.

BRIAN   You wanna do it again? You can't really tell if she's alive, anyway. Not with all that blood 'n shit on her . . .

BRENT *crouches down and touches the body. Lifts one of her lifeless arms.*

BRENT   No, people can tell. They'll know. Frame by frame and all that shit . . .

BRIAN   Right . . .

BRENT   Pisses me off . . .

BRIAN   . . . I did say something . . .

BRENT   I KNOW! (*Beat.*) I heard you, man. It's my fault . . . *mine*. It's just . . . (*Thinks.*) Wait. What about pissing on her or something of that nature? Taking a dump, maybe . . .

BRIAN   No, we did that already . . .

BRENT   What? When?

BRIAN   Not her, but that other one. The redhead.

BRENT   Oh, fuck. Right. Yeah.

BRENT *thinks for a minute. Goes over to a wire basket that's near a computer. Digs through it.*

BRENT   Didn't we . . . (*Looking.*) I thought I . . .? We've had requests for watching someone do it with a dead girl, right? I'd *swear* we have!

BRIAN   Ummm, yeah, I think.

BRENT   I *know* we have. Right?

BRIAN   Probably. People are weird.

BRENT   So then . . .

BRIAN   Not me, dude. You go ahead . . .

BRENT   Why?

BRIAN   That's not . . .

BRENT   What?

BRIAN   . . . I don't wanna get blood all over my dick and stuff. That's gross.

BRENT   Oh, you don't mind us killing somebody but now it's like, what? A *moral* thing with you . . . or some *sanitary* deal?

BRIAN   I dunno. Maybe. I mean, she's . . . all . . .

BRENT   You pussy! She's *dead* . . . not like she's gonna feel anything. (*Beat.*) Every girl I ever dated, at some point I wished she was fucking dead—it'll be just like that!

BRIAN   No, man, I don't care about the religion of it or whatever, I just don't wanna be up in some . . . cold . . . you know. That's all.

BRENT   Fuck! Fine. I'm a better camera operator than you are, but fine . . .

BRIAN   Still . . . come on, man . . . that's nasty.

BRENT   Whatever! Nice *friend* . . .

BRIAN Sorry!

BRENT Fine! Just get the digi-cam and point it at us, can you do that much?

BRIAN 'Course. I am sorry, but I'm not . . .

BRENT Just grab it and hurry! Go!!

BRIAN *runs and grabs up a video camera as* BRENT *drops his jeans around his shoes. Kneels.*

BRENT From the front?

BRIAN Nah, go for it from behind. Gonna see more of her face that way . . . could look pretty cool.

BRENT That's true. Good one . . . (*On his knees.*) Ok, and ready? DEAD GIRL GETTING FUCKED. Take one. (*Enters her.*) She's still warm, dude. You're missing out.

BRENT *laughs at this, shakes the camera.*

BRIAN Sorry. Fuck! I wrecked that one . . . *don't* make me laugh! Start over.

BRENT Douchebag! Come on! (*Smiles.*) This is very serious, you prick. It's money . . . (*Trying to be serious.*) DEAD GIRL GETTING FUCKED. REAR ENTRY. Take one . . .

BRIAN *laughs again, dropping to the floor with the camera in his hands.*

BRIAN BITCH! Don't add "rear entry" or I will keep laughing!

BRENT Stop! (*Laughing.*) Come on, this isn't fun.

BRIAN Ok, go. Just do it and stop adding shit.

BRENT Ok, fine. DEAD GIRL GETTING FUCKED. FROM BEHIND.

BRIAN Dude!

BRENT Stop!

BRIAN *You* stop!! Asshole! (*Filming.*) Now go!!

BRIAN *kneels down, filming the* GIRL'*s face.* BRENT *begins to fuck her from behind. Some blood spills out her mouth.*

BRENT Is it good? How's it look, fucker?

BRIAN Ohhh! You just, like, pumped blood out of her mouth! No way!! *Awesome . . .*

BRENT You get it?

BRIAN 'Course! Do it again!!

BRENT *stops, out of breath. Leans over, pulling some of her hair away from her face. Studies her face. Glances over at his friend.*

BRENT . . . hey, look. I think she likes me!

They laugh together at this. Like boys do. Loud and hard. After a moment, BRENT *starts pumping her body again. His friend keeps filming.*

BRIAN It looks great! Keep going!

BRENT (*Grabbing her hand.*) Wave to the folks at home, sweetie! (*Waving her hand.*) That's it, yeah! Wave to the nice people, bitch . . . that's it, yeah, that's it! Wave! Wave!! WAVE, YOU CUNT!!! (*Waving her hand.*) *WAVE*!!!!

BRENT *keeps fucking her and waving her hand.* BRIAN *keeps laughing and filming.*

Sudden burst of ear-shattering music.

Silence. Darkness.

THE UNIMAGINABLE

THE UNIMAGINABLE had its world premiere as part of the "TERROR!" festival at Southwark Playhouse in London, England, in October 2010. It was directed by Jason Lawson.

VOICE   Scott Christie

Silence. Darkness.

A hint of light reveals a pile of dolls lying on the floor. Left in a heap.
Garish faces. Blood slowly drips on them from above.

A whisper somewhere in the room. Nearby. Amplified.

VOICE . . . I don't know how you do it. I really don't. I mean, look at
'em. Take a long look at them faces and I'll say it again. I-do-not-
know-how-you-do-it. Leave 'em alone, go out at night. Dinner. To
the theater. Here. With me. Listening. Sure they're alright, locked
up in your safe little houses or your fancy flats high up in the sky—
but you know they're not. In your guts, deep deep in those fat
bellies of yours, you know they're not. Every day that you send
them off to school, down to the shops or to a friend's house so
that you can run out and get your hair done . . . you know inside
that you've opened up the door for someone like me. For the likes
of me. (*A tiny laugh.*) That's beautiful, that kind of trust—it's not
anything a person can win over or gain or whatever. It just gets
handed out, you simply put them into our hands and that's that.
You don't think twice about it—and you are surrounded by us.
That's what you don't seem to understand, as many times as it
happens, every instance you read of it in the papers and yet you
turn around and send the little dears off with the nanny or out to
the park or on a plane to meet their grandparents at Disney
World—and one by one, we pick them off. Separate 'em from the
herd and then we strike . . . we swoop in and grab them and off
we go. With your loved ones. Your little little gorgeous bundles of

joy. And when we do, when that moment happens—I want you to know something. That second, that instant when they become ours—hidden away in our lorries or basements or an old irrigation ditch somewhere until we decide what to do with 'em—from that minute on, they will never know love again. Or kindness. Or the warm touch of a parent's embrace. Not ever. So remember that as you read the ransom note or stare at the telly waiting for news as the police and your neighbors bravely walk through the fields and back alleys surrounding your homes, just know that. Your terrified little children are in our clutches and will feel nothing but pain and sadness and terror for the last hours of their lives. Because of you. It was you that signed the permission slip for the school trip or said "Yes" to that pizza party they walked over to and were never seen again. *It was only two doors down*! I know. I know it was, but in those fifty feet from your house to the store, we grabbed them up, snatched them away to a place you've never even imagined until today, this moment—and now it's here. It has happened, the unimaginable, and that is all you've got left: is to imagine it. Well, imagine this: what you've done, by trusting me. Someone like me. For letting them out-of-doors at just the wrong time, at that moment when we were passing by. Or waiting. Waiting just for them. And now we've done it . . . ruined their little life and so it's into a bag or a suitcase or just the dirty ground itself; we hide 'em away and off we go, out on the prowl one more time because we can't stop, no, we don't want to stop and we won't stop, no we won't. (*A little laugh.*) Why should we? It's your fault, you gave 'em up, let them go and now they're ours, ours to do with as we please and pleased we are at what they'll do for us. Such awful things then on we go to the next one. And the next. And the next. Maybe yours this time—no, never, it's always someone else's problem, isn't it? Isn't it?—Don't make me laugh. Who are you kidding now? We'll get yours. We will.

And when we do? Imagine the very worst. Don't worry, it will be. The very most horrific shit you could ever imagine in those pretty little heads of yours. But occasionally one gets away, you say, one may slip through our fingers or a broken window and they make it back home to you and their family. It happens. They survive and that is true. But do know this: they will never be the same again. Their life will be filled with nightmares and bad, bad love and faces looming at them out of the crowd and maybe even killing themselves because that's all there is left, it's the only way out, the only way, the only way to get out of their very own heads. So one way or the other, we'll get them. We take them from you and there's nothing you can do. Just watch. And wait. Knowing they'll be dug up or pulled from a pond today or next week or when you're fifty, but until then you won't know, you can't know and you will fear the worst, hope for the best but in your heart, that hard hard little suburban heart of yours you will know the truth: they're gone but not gone, dead but not yet dead. They are truly the undead. (*A tiny laugh.*) Isn't it silly that we grow up afraid of the dark? The dark is safe, no one can find you in the dark, you can hide and run and get away—it's the light that always ruins it for us. It catches us out or gives up our position or, yes, exposes us in the end. Not dark-ness. No, never that. But our parents tell us to be afraid of silly things like zombies & dragons & negroes & the boogeyman but all the while they are surrounded by monsters, real live monsters like me and him and him and her and they send their children out in our midst and one by one, off they go. Lost. Missing. Abducted. That's what is happening to them, so teach your children, you teach 'em that, why don't you? The truth. Teach them about what is truly unimaginable. Imagine it now or soon it may be too late. In fact, for someone tonight, maybe even someone here, watching this, it already is. Can you *imagine* that? (*A little laugh.*) Well, I can. Every stinking inch of it. You're already reaching for your phones, aren't you? Just to be safe. One tiny call to the sitter and all will be well. So you think. So you know. So says your mum and dad and all that you believe in. But if you call, if you do, if you give in to your fear right now—and the phone keeps ringing, no one picks up, for whatever reason, what then? Tell me that, you pretty lady or handsome man, tell me what will you do then? In that moment when you start to panic and your eyes widen, that is what I live to see. That is the moment that I love. So do it, give in, go for it and make that call. Try and squelch your fears right now. I beg you. Go on, I do. I-beg-you-to. Who knows? Maybe that'll work. Maybe everything is fine. (*Beat.*) Or *maybe* . . . (*A tiny laugh.*) Go on. I dare you to . . .

The VOICE *gives off a tiny laugh again, then it's gone.*

Music overtakes the scene and punishes us in our seats.

Silence. Darkness.

TOTALLY

TOTALLY had its world premiere as part of "Seven Card Draw" (a collection of short plays) at Dixon Place in New York City in March 2010. It was directed by Carolyn Cantor.

GIRL   Piper Perabo

Silence. Darkness.

Lights up on a GIRL. *Lovely. Standing there. Waiting.*

GIRL . . . oh, hey, hi, how's it going? (*Beat.*) Hmmmm? Me? Oh, you
know, I've been . . . I dunno, it's been interesting. Uh-huh. *Very* interesting. Totally. I'm not really feeling so—I mean, I'm supposed to
meet someone so I can't stand around and, but ok, lemme just . . .
I'll tell you the highlights. How's that? If I just skim it for now and
then maybe we'll catch up at some other, whenever. Maybe I can
text you or we can skype or, or—yeah. We can do that another
time. Cool. Great. (*Beat.*) *So.* My birthday, right? In January—and
yes, you missed it, bitch, thanks, I even sent you an *e-vite* for it,
you never responded—well, ends up being this huge day for me
but, I mean, like, starting out, when I'm waking up that morning,
how could I ever even know that? You know? So yes, it's a big
deal, party that I throw myself every year; it's worth it, I get to see
people *and* the presents—not why I do it but it doesn't suck—and
just a chance to, you know, keep in touch with everybody, for us
to keep it real. Nice. So, yeah, that happens and I drink too much
and Douglas, you know him, right, of course you do . . . *everyone*
knows Douglas apparently, that's what I find out that night. He
gets me a necklace from Tiffany's which is lovely, it is, very whatever, lovely . . . and they've put the receipt in there so I pull it out,
just to get it out of the way so I can admire the jewelry—seriously,
I'm not at all *studying* it or anything like he starts accusing me of
—and it's tucked in there, right? It's just his receipt to the present,

but on it is charges for, I mean, like, two other necklaces. *Two* more of these things. *Exact* same ones. And so you know how that goes, it blows up into this whole . . . shit, whatever you'd expect, with all the lying about they're for his mom and, and his sister for their, like, upcoming *birthdays*—yeah, right, in April and November—and then it just spills out of him. Like, plop, wham, on the table . . . yeah. He's been messing around and he's seeing someone—one does turn out to be for his sister which is whatever —why he has to buy it during a trip to get me my gift, I don't know, but still, it's his family, at least—but yes, there's this girl and "it's over," he promises, just bought her this as a goodbye thing. I'm, you can imagine, I am knocked out. Flat. I'm planning to *marry* this guy, make a life with him and this is going on? All this time, however long? With *packages* and shit, too, not just fucking her and stuff, like guys sometimes do because of all that excess energy, but really . . . I'm dead inside. Suddenly I feel like I went outside and ate up all the dog shit that I'm able to find out there on the street. That's how I feel. (*Beat.*) Because, see . . . *I* had a gift for him that night, too. I'm ready to tell him, yeah—I have something all prepared for the evening and now he's gone and, like, ruined it. You think I'm gonna tell him I'm pregnant now? Are you crazy? Huh? That's—I mean, I dunno, and maybe some girls even would, what better time to get him back on the straight and whatever, but see, he's always so worried about that, he is, he's this Mr. Protection Freak with the, like, *double* condoms and making sure I'm caught up on my pills and whatever. Yeah. Like, *insane* about it to a point where I'm already nervous that he'll deny it or won't even believe it's his, and plus there's this other part of me that I get from my dad, this sort of deep-rooted stubborn streak—one whole side of me is now thinking, "Screw you,

Douglas, you don't get to know this! No, it's my secret now, bitch, and you're out in the cold!" (*Beat.*) Do you need to go? No? Okay, cool. Yeah, so, anyhow, that's what I'm feeling inside, up in my head . . . but see, in the moment, I get all soft. I go ahead and cry and beg him to come back and we make up and all that shit— I do really believe he's done with this girl, this "Melody" something and he even has the nerve to call her up and put us on the phone together! Wants her to say it to me, that they're done and she does, whether she believes it or not, she did say it, so—and on the surface, I mean, as far as he can tell, we're fine. We are totally good and all is well in the bell tower. But— (*Phone rings.*) Wait, lemme just check, see if this is . . . (*She answers it.*) Hello? Yeah, I'm at the, no, I'm already here. Yep. I'm just standing here, so . . . ok. Yes, *ok,* alright, got it. I'll meet you here . . . 'bye. (*Puts her cell away.*) Sorry. I hate it when someone else does that but it really was important. I told you, I think, that I'm meeting some-body. Didn't I? Yeah, I'm pretty sure I mentioned it. (*Beat.*) And so that's been me, for, like, the last few months, I've just been . . . wandering around with this, this, like . . . *knowledge* in my head and I'm wanting to, I guess, maybe, do something. To risk it all, everything I have or expect to get, my happiness, to pay it back to him. To let him have it. A *taste,* right? Of his own whatever . . . medicine and shit, or however that saying goes. What's that thing they used to say, way back when to people who were, you know, avenging loved ones or fighting those mythical animals and all that? Hmmmm? Oh, come on, you know! It's . . . "payback's a bitch!" That's the one. And hey, it's so fucking true: Payback is a bad-ass bitch. (*Beat.*) And, so, yeah, that's what I'm doing. I mean, in life. And also now. Right now, that's what I am doing here in about a few minutes . . . yep. See, what I did—and this is wrong,

I know that, and normally, you could put your purse down right there . . . go off to the bathroom all day long and I would not think of touching it. Looking inside. And it's the same for my boyfriend. *Totally* true. He used to leave his computer open and on the, like, *Swimsuit Edition* page and I would stroll right past, couldn't care less, my show's on. Seriously. But now—shit, *now* it's a war, with me slinking around and digging through his sock drawer or his wallet if he's stupid enough to leave it around and . . . just a bunch of crazy shit like that. Looking for names or, or, or clues or something. Somebody that I can blame all this stuff on, march up to their door and pound on it, make some big fucking scene out there on their porch for the neighbors to see. *That's* where my head is at because of a little Tiffany's necklace—not even any diamonds in it or anything—but that's how I'm feeling as I'm sitting there in a panic with his address book open in my lap, me trying to decipher every name or set of initials like I'm some . . . and then it strikes me. Like a bolt, blazing down from the sky above—maybe not Heaven but some place up there—and zapping me right in the fucking face. Bam! Zap! You know? Oww! Shit. Stupid ol' me. It's been right here, *staring* at me, the whole damn time. The solution to what I'm feeling here and needing. You know. To make things right, I mean. (*Beat.*) It's not her I care about. It's him. My Douglas. He's the one needs to pay for this shit, true? Not any girl I spoke to for five seconds on the phone one night—I don't care about her. Nope. It's Douglas. So I decide, "Ok, so you're so worried about us using protection"—not right now, though, 'cause I did tell him about the baby and, surprise, he's, like, completely excited about it. Yeah, he is. Totally. So he's treating me like a tiny little fragile thing, opening doors for me and lifting shit and whatever, I don't mind, it's new to me—*but* this is how I figure it's all gotta go, so that by the time the kid comes we'll be even. (*Beat.*) I copied all the numbers in his little book there—we have one of those faxes that also do the copies, it's nice—and I'm going down the list, guy by guy, in pretty much alphabetical order, I mean, unless I know for sure that he's an ugly person or fat or whatever, a hairy back, maybe—and I'm fucking them. Once each. Name by name. And you know what, what's really shocking to me but actually not that much because you know why? Guys are pretty much whores, they really are—women are the ones who get that word thrown at 'em but it's really guys who're mostly that way—for being his "friends" or so they say, it's amazing how many of them are *totally* into what I'm doing. I mean, as long as you promise there's no strings and it's just a fuck and that's all—most of 'em say "hell yeah!" and are in my pants before I finish explaining it to 'em! It's pretty . . . well, I find it all kinda amusing. I do. Totally. (*Beat.*) And that's what I'm up to. Meeting one of my guys here in a minute. Yep . . . I've only been at it a little while and I'm already into the "K's." So. I mean, I've had to pick the pace up a little because it was hard in that first trimester with all the—(*She makes a puking sound.*)—but I've kicked it into gear and it's going really good. Fast. Not sure I'll get through the whole alphabet but I'm gonna go for it, trying to finish it off before the kid comes. It's a boy, we already know, so there's that. (*Beat.*) Oh, God, should I not've—is this something you didn't wanna know? Sorry. You okay? Because I sometimes have a real big mouth and I probably should've said something first before getting all . . . Oh. Oh, shit, wait. No. Sorry! I know, I get it. Don't even say anything. Your fiancé, his last name starts with . . . honestly and I mean totally honest here: I never, and I mean *ever,* even considered him. I did not. I mean, hey, it's me, I'm not gonna suddenly get all—I *know* who's off-limits and who's not. I promise. Promise. Yeah . . . *Totally.* (*She looks away, checking her watch.*) Anyway, I should get . . . right. I've still got some errands to run after this and I wanna be home to cook Douglas dinner. He puts in a long day over at the Nissan so he's— that probably seems weird, right, with what I'm doing, but it works in my head so, screw it, you know, I just keep going with it! Whatever, right? Totally. Yeah, so . . . oh, I think I see him coming now, over there, by the . . . (*She waves.*) I gotta go but we should do something! Little spa action or, you know, before the kid comes. And I wanna hear about you, too, I do! Here I am, going on and on and on but I am dying to know what you've been up to. Ok? So call me, we'll grab a bite or, or . . . whatever, go tanning, if you want. Wait, maybe that's bad for the baby? Shit, I'm not even sure—I've been, like, six times since I got pregnant, so . . . maybe we just do lunch for now, 'kay? Great! Perfect. I'm . . . (*Waving.*) I'll be right there! (*To us again.*) Don't tell anybody, it's Doug's cousin, Tommy, who I've always had this little thing for. I didn't even call him. I swear! I guess he just heard from somebody: he sent me a text and here we are. Go figure. Anyway! I'm off, let's keep in touch or something—God, I love what you did to your hair. Honestly, the bangs! I mean, they look awesome. So cute. Really. (*Realizes.*) Oh shit, I didn't even tell, fuck, the whole . . . *this* is the funny part! I mean, the like, you know, *Twilight Zone* bit or whatever. The zinger. So I'm going at it with his friends and all that, like I said, and I go in for my next check-up, doing what I'm supposed to, ok, so I'm up in the stirrups there—doctor looks at me (it's a man, which I hate but he's my mom's guy and I've been going there for years and years so I just figure whatever, right?) and he's all up in there and pressing my tummy and stuff, a look on his face of I'm not sure what. He studies my chart, takes another feel up inside me—I have not shaved in, like, a *month,* but what're you gonna do?—and he finally says, "Huh. I get the feeling we are totally off on this, and I mean by, like, a couple of months. I think you're only in the first trimester *now.*" (*Beat.*) *What?* He's not at all sure what's up, thinks maybe I first got pregnant, then lost it, and now maybe . . . I'm up into the "E's" and "F's" by this time and I do not want to hear this! But yeah. He tells me I might not've even been pregnant the first time! It happens . . . or whatever. So, how's *that* for karma? Huh? I mean, like, just *totally* weird. Right? Totally.

She waves again to someone in the distance.

GIRL Alright, I'm really leaving this time but let's do it, get together and . . . you pick. And next time, it's *all* you, I promise. My mouth is—(*Pretends to zip her lips.*)—no, I mean that! *Totally.* I do! (*Grins.*) You shut up, I honestly *do!* Bitch. (*Beat.*) Ok, wish me luck, 'cause I hear he's . . . totally! What's the saying? Men: they're hell on the forearms, tough on the knees! (*Beat.*) Maybe it's not a saying, I dunno, maybe that was just my mom going on about—anyway, who knows? We shall see, right? (*Beat.*) What? Oh, this? (*She points to her neck.*) Yeah, it's nice, huh? Pretty. No, you're right. I mean, as necklaces go . . . (*Beat.*) Anyhoo! I'm outta here. Call me. And your hair's . . . I love it. No, I do. I *do!* God, I *really* do! Bitch. (*She smiles.*) I totally do. Yeah. (*Smiles again.*) *Totally!*

A last smile. She turns and waves offstage. Only now do we see how big her belly really is. She is noticeably great with child.

She trots off and disappears into the shadows.

Silence. Darkness.

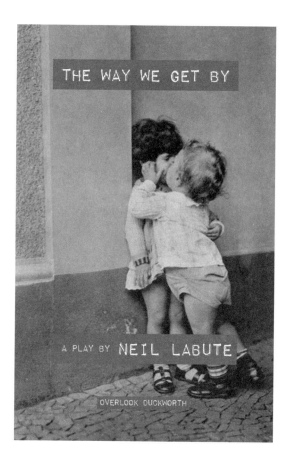

New York. Middle of the night. Now.

Meet Beth and Doug: two people who have no problem getting dates with their partners of choice. What they do have is an awkward encounter after spending one hit night together following a drunken wedding reception.

Slyly profound and irresistibly passionate, *The Way We Get By* is Neil LaBute's audacious tale of a very modern romance—a sharp, sexy, fresh look at love and lust and the whole damn thing.

"Viscerally romantic, almost shockingly sensitive, even, dare we say it, sweet . . . LaBute . . . dares here to explore less obviously explosive territory. Yet, somehow, this daring feels deep." —**Linda Winer**, *Newsday*

$14.95 978-1-4683-1208-9

THE OVERLOOK PRESS • NEW YORK • WWW.OVERLOOKPRESS.COM

Karen and Steve are glamorous movie stars with one thing in common: desperation. How far will they let themselves go to keep from slipping further down the Hollywood food chain?

Sexy, daring, darkly hilarious—and Neil LaBute's first officially billed comedy—*The Money Shot* lands as sharp and hot as a paparazzo's camera flash in a starlet's eye.

"A wickedly funny new comedy."   **—Jennifer Farrar, Associated Press**

$14.95   978-1-4683-0722-1

"THE MOST LEGITIMATELY PROVOCATIVE AND POLARIZING PLAYWRIGHT AT WORK TODAY." —DAVID AMSDEN, *NEW YORK*

REASONS TO BE HAPPY

A PLAY BY
NEIL LaBUTE

OVERLOOK

In the companion piece to Neil LaBute's 2009 Tony-nominated *Reasons to be Pretty*, Greg, Steph, Carly, and Kent pick up their lives three years later, but in different romantic pairings, as they each search desperately for that elusive object of desire: happiness.

"Mr. LaBute is more relaxed as a playwright than he's ever been. He is clearly having a good time revisiting old friends . . . you're likely to feel the same way . . . the most winning romantic comedy of the summer, replete with love talk, LaBute-style, which isn't so far from hate talk . . . "   **—Ben Brantley, *The New York Times***

In this electrifying two-hander, the young and beautiful Velvet and the older, volatile Fred revisit a shared history, and as power shifts and tension mounts, the twisted heart of their relationship is slowly revealed in a stunning climax. This volume contains the stage version of this work, which is also a film directed by Neil LaBute, with Stanley Tucci and Alice Eve.

"*Some Velvet Morning* is provocation of the most artful kind." —*The Village Voice*

$14.95 978-1-4683-0916-4